Musings of a One-Time Atheist

Multiple Sclerosis:
              Life, Love, Faith and . . . .

    how to make a bed

Vernon Lewis © 2024

All rights reserved. No part of this publication may be reproduced, stored in a retrieval system or transmitted in any form or by any means – electronic, mechanical, photocopy, recording or any other – except for brief quotations in printed reviews, without the prior permission of the publisher.

Paperback ISBN 978-1-923225-62-6
Ebook ISBN 978-0-6451378-2-8
Audiobook ISBN 978-0-6451378-4-2

All substantial quotations are used with permission of the authors

Preface

This book is called "Musings . . . ." for a very good reason. That's what it is.

In some ways, it is a series of essays on whatever topic I fancy to discuss. Just as importantly, the material discussed has a clear undercurrent of my current beliefs. One major point I make on several occasions is that the beliefs I now hold are not mutually exclusive of someone reading this book or the Bible without gaining much of value as a basis for making important decisions about one's own life; one can read the Bible without being a Christian. What is more, the Bible is now available in translations which are much easier to understand than the old King James version. (That of course is still the only one of truth for some. Not me.)

There are also some aspects of my life which are not discussed. You don't need to know everything about me.

For the same reason I do not make any public dedication of this book.

I do want to thank lots of people who helped me along the way. They know who they are so they do not need any public acknowledgement. The only exception is Paul Teague who provided much assistance in the process of getting these musings into a useful form.

Thank you to God very much for providing support along the way; from being there when I was about to commit suicide to being responsible for inviting me to the critical events in my life to bringing my thinking up short when I was heading down the wrong burrow. When I look back, I can see the course of events in a new light; perhaps there was something else happening of which I was not aware at the time. That is the guide for the substance of this book and my musings.

The diagnosis of MS was the switch point for me; before and after make for the different direction my life took. The material included was written intermittently from 2012 to 2020 with final editing and printing in 2021. The main reason for the disjointed nature of my application was my displacement to write another book with Paul which dealt with some major issues for our community, including fraud and dishonesty. My ideas continued to develop so they are fairly much what I hold at publication.

I have had the opportunity to spend much time, it seems to me, in reflection on important issues of life, and death. The time when I have been in hospital with nothing much to do, in waiting rooms while I wait to see another medical expert and, in many hours, awake at night. What is more is that I have had people around me, or have sought them out, who have provided many different ideas for me to consider and choose to incorporate them into my life, or not. That diagnosis of MS was a major stimulus for re-consideration of what life was really all about. I have reached a point of peace and acceptance of what is, what might be or what I could change. There is one thing I would very much like to change: it is not my decision to make so I can only hope. I love my life, even with all its vicissitudes. It's the only one I have so I will make the best of it that I can.

Additional note for the second printing: 2022 was a year I would cheerfully expunge. I had five visits to hospital with a variety of complaints, none relating to MS. It has meant that I am only just regaining the energy to do more about making this book more widely available. Life is becoming much more liveable and it is the exercises taught by physiotherapists, which are having the best effect. I can now stand and turn, so that I can transfer from one place to sit to another.

Contents

Preface 3
Prologue 9
Events along the way 10
Enter an evangelist 11
Adventures with MS 15
Give it a go, mate. What is success to you? 39
And this is why 61
Make it right the first time! 80
You want what? 94
Do you want more? 114
Encounters with God 135
Epilogue 156
Poems 158
   My Loving Prayer 158
   Headlights in the Sky 159
   You and Me 161
   I can stay here no longer 162
   Walls 163
   Road to Copperlode Dam 164
   Gillies Highway 165
   Lines at sundown looking over Atherton 166
   In Church, 25/01/09 167
   Ode to the sheet 169
   Metaphor 171

Prologue

It was a blinding flash of understanding.

It was October, 1980 and I was standing in the kitchen and surveying the wooded gully of which we, with the bank, had just bought two acres. Nestling under the tree canopy were numerous houses, most of which gave only a hint of their existence.

I was a teacher of Classical Studies, among other things, and I realised that the myths of the ancient Greeks and Romans contained numerous gods to meet the needs of the people in whatever way they saw fit. Those gods had all been creations of men.

If gods were a creation of men, then god had no real substance at all, so there must be no real gods.

Ergo, I am an atheist.

It really was a blinding flash of understanding.

Events along the way

October 1980	Blinding flash – I'm an atheist
August 20 1989	Diagnosis of MS
Sometime 1997-9	Enter an Evangelist
Easter 2000	Decision to go to church, sing
Later in 2000	Move out of home
Even later in 2000	Death of mother
Later still	Return to family home
2005	Separation from wife
	Death of Mother-in-Law
2007	Move to Cairns
Nov 14, 2013	Move to Adelaide
Dec 29, 2013	2nd Marriage
Easter 2020	Move to aged residential accommodation

Enter an evangelist

I could not believe it was me doing this! I wasn't one of those Wackos who went forward when the preacher invited everyone to. I did not do this! I couldn't stop myself. At least only a few people knew me here! And there were some others who had done the same thing. I wasn't the only one.

This was the most important encounter I ever had with Jesus/God.

I grovelled on the floor at the foot of the low stage at the end of a row of those others who had also come forward. Eventually the speaker reached me. He reached down and put his hand on my head, saying, "You don't think you can do this, do you."

My head shook vigorously and rapidly from side to side in agreement with him as I continued looking down.

He went on to say some other things about which I am not certain. I knew, however, that from then on, I was a Christian.

It was some time in the late 1990's.

Some background to set the scene for this makes it even more incredible, in the true sense of that word. My family and I had returned to Adelaide from Port Lincoln since it became clear that I could not continue as a Drama teacher. Port Lincoln High School needed a teacher of Drama and had Computing teachers aplenty.

My retraining as a teacher of Computing was therefore of no value to Port Lincoln High School. A short visit to hospital after the Year 12 Drama performance for assessment was more than enough to convince us that, while Port Lincoln had been a wonderful place to live, our time there had to come to an end if I was to survive in a healthy way. MS and stressful exercise did not mix.

After settling in to a home in Adelaide, I sought advice from a friend as to where she might be singing. I had a background of classical training in singing and felt the need to continue in a less formal way than as part of an established major choir or opera company. She suggested a group that had a Christian mission. As an atheist I was reluctant to enter into the full range of the rehearsal activities. I tried to arrive late and sneak out early, the idea being to avoid the "religious stuff". I was successful sometimes. Eventually, after two performances in a suburban shopping centre, I decided that I could not continue since my public appearances as part of a Christian group were not acceptable for my family or me.

The woman who led the group maintained contact from time to time and she invited me to attend a meeting that was to be addressed by a former Commissioner of the Sri Lankan Broadcasting Commission. As a former teacher of Media Studies, I was interested in gaining a greater insight into the operation of a government media organisation. Unfortunately, or perhaps it was fortunately, he was speaking as an evangelist rather than a Commissioner! I stayed because I thought it good manners to do so. Similarly, I listened to what he had to say and joined in the prayer at the end of his address. He invited anyone who felt they wanted a deeper relationship with Christ to raise their hand. (All eyes closed; all heads bowed. Be anonymous.) My right hand was up high; I don't do this! I could not drag it down. Then the invitation to come forward. . . . .

How time (and God) has a way of changing things.

Adventures with MS[1]

Friday, August 20, 1989. The neurologist walked into the Orthopaedic ward where I was and said, "You're too sick to do the last couple of tests we wanted to do but we're pretty confident you have MS. The best thing to do is to go home and get on with your life." He then left.

'That means wheelchair, and who knows." Aghast might the best word to describe how I felt at that time. I was lost. I felt really crook. I was still suffering the effects of the allergic reaction to the drugs they injected into my spine. And I had no-one to talk too.

I was lucky. The "sister", as she was known then, had a few words and pointed me in the direction of the MS Society. Somehow, other people in my family (Mother, brothers and their wives) got to hear about the diagnosis and my return flight to Port Lincoln was arranged. At least I would be with my wife and kids again.

---

[1] MS is that neurological complaint where the fatty tissue of the myelin sheath enclosing the central nervous system becomes inflamed and then scarred. The effect is to muddle the nerve signals passing between the brain and the rest of the body. The name, *Multiple Sclerosis,* translates into Many Scars in simple language. That doesn't sound so good when you are naming a complaint though. Cause is unknown and there is very limited, symptomatic treatment. Symptoms . . . I'll include that later.

Just to back pedal a bit. Well, 18 months actually. 1988 was a terrible year for me, in spite of all the preparations for the sesquicentenary (150th anniversary) of the European settlement of Port Lincoln.

It started with a freak cloudburst, on the Friday of the first week of term one, just before I rode my bike to work at Port Lincoln High School. My route took me down a very steep street to a T-junction with a major traffic carriageway, particularly at that time. I was going too fast, then the brakes refused to grip; calliper brakes are not very reliable when wet because the water is like a lubricant. I could only see the cross road in one direction. The other was obscured by a concrete wall. I had no choice, I thought. Straight ahead was a footpath and a horizontal pipe railing, to stop people falling into the lower level of the building below. I did not fancy hitting that at speed. I deliberately put the bike on the ground. Ouch!!!

I wrecked my shirt and, apparently, dislocated my shoulder and had it go back on its own. I went on to school to deal with the first commitment of the day and then organised to go home to get cleaned up before returning to take the rest of the day's classes. I got to see a doctor who sent me home with a firm direction and a certificate. The specialist was next on the list and he gave me the rest of term 1 on sick leave. That was stupid: I was perfectly capable of teaching at least some of my classes; at least those for which I could not give much assistance to a fill-in teacher. Of particular concern were my Media Studies classes. After the initial pain and shock was over, I had only the slight problem of a shoulder that needed to be rested in a sling with a regular dose of Paracetamol for the discomfort. Nonetheless, I was told not to appear at work until the next term.

We had just bought a house and planned to make some changes to the back garden. First was the installation of a lawn, which involved a pop-up sprinkler watering system, a hole for a new trampoline, the construction of three swings and then, of course, the planting. We had a contractor dig the hole for the trampoline and do the excavations to create the sloping soil for the lawn. I then used a grubber, or mattock, to dig the trenches for the pop-up sprinklers, using only my right arm and hand. I also made use of previous experience to install the pipes and sprinklers with the wiring for automatic control. That at least turned out very well. The swing was also created and became the source of much enjoyment for our children and their friends.

While I was acting deputy principal for the second term, it was not a pleasant experience. That is extraneous to the story and what is relevant is the second half of the year when we were to take long service leave until two weeks before the end of year. We arranged all of the details so that we could travel to Brisbane, staying in overnight vans on the way and then in Brisbane to stay with my brother. The two weeks when we went to the World Expo and also to Fraser Island was very pleasant. Leaving Brisbane and travelling to Sydney was less than pleasant. I suspect there is some lingering confusion from that. It need not concern us further here.

What is of relevance is that I was seeking a career change and had made an appointment with an ABC TV Executive Producer in Sydney to discuss a proposal for a documentary on European settlement on the Eyre Peninsula from the point of view of the displaced indigenous peoples. That interview did not go well. "Come back when you have a script". For a documentary???

We returned to Adelaide and Port Lincoln staying with family and friends along the way. (By the end of the year the ABC had made a documentary of European settlement from the indigenous people's point of view in the Sydney area, the home of the ABC.) I was at a loss as to what to do. I was given much encouragement to attempt to create a script of sorts and proceed as best I could, with or without the support of the ABC.

I went blind in one eye!

Optician and Doctor friends climbed inside my eye (at least that is what it felt like) and could not find a satisfactory diagnosis. Perhaps it was a torn retina. Off to Adelaide by plane to see an ophthalmologist. He climbed further inside my eye and could not make a confident diagnosis. Fly home, still blind in my left eye. Then the sight returned!

Yippee! I would be able to see to direct the filming of the documentary, with dramatic re-enactments, I had organised; to be associated with the re-enactment of the first landing on the foreshore of the City. Strange. Walking to the locations for the filming of significant events and standing while I directed the filming became difficult. My legs did not want to work the way they used to. That fatigue got worse. I decided that I would get the video into the form ready for broadcast, show it to the cast of over 300 locals and then sort out what was going on. It was now into 1989.

I could not stand to present the final product or the selection of "bloopers".

I went to another Doctor friend (It was in a small city of about 13,000 people). Blood test and referral to another specialist, neurologist this time, when he next visited the city. Told to make an appointment with the Royal Adelaide Hospital for a week of tests! In hospital for tests? For a week? Seemed everybody was trying not to be concerned. All except me! Off to Adelaide again.

First test; a myelogram. Local anaesthetic did not touch the pain of the needle into the spinal space between the vertebrae. (Now they do a painless MRI which did not exist then.) Back to the ward lying flat on my back until next afternoon. Only then was I to start sitting up.

I vomited!

They sat me up some more, the standard solution to vomiting.

I vomited more.

They sat me up further.

I vomited more.

They tried to make contact with the specialist. He was not in his rooms or at home. I continued to retch and they maintained the upward aspect of my torso.

Until they located him, at last. (No mobile phones in 1989). "Lie him down, flat on his back again. (This is a known possible reaction to the dye used in the injection.)" (Pity I was in an orthopaedic ward rather than a neurology one.) Oh, the relief. No more retching. Relax!

The time from that Tuesday until the Friday morning is a blur of trying to stand to have showers, different tests of eyesight, balance and whatever else, I know not. And much lying flat on my back. In there somewhere are phone calls to my wife and to some of my siblings and mother. Eventually I arranged to leave hospital on the next Monday and fly home.

I still could not sit up without feeling nauseous. I was lucky. The plane was fully booked except for one seat. That meant I could have two seats to myself. The airline brought me out from the terminal in a wheelchair and used a lift to get me up to the plane. I was put in place before the other passengers boarded. It felt really strange to be half lying on the seats saying hello to all the people I knew, walking past me to their seat!

It felt just as strange to still be half lying over the two seats as they all left the plane in Port Lincoln. When it came time for me to alight, I was supported from the aircraft to the car by my wife and a former Miss Australia. She had been the Narrator in the drama documentary which I had just completed and was at the airport to collect her son, returning from Adelaide. I felt very privileged indeed. She would not have thought a thing about it. She was a person helping a friend. Double privilege.

It was at least six weeks before I could walk confidently with my head up. I remember teaching my Year 11 Drama class from my lounge room floor after their parents had organised the sharing of driving to my home for the purpose. There followed a term on stress leave as I disputed with the Education Department over the details of my re-training. A satisfactory result was achieved and I returned to work in the second term. Further disputes! Over my means of transport within the grounds, from the staff room at the "bottom" of the school to the Drama Room at the very "top".[2] Resolved satisfactorily so I could ride my "nifty 50" Honda scooter. I had bought this for the purpose of getting to and from work, around the school, including Yard duty, and around the golf course with a friend who rode a small motorbike towing a buggy.

1990 was spent studying 0.3 time and teaching 0.7. 1991 saw a review and I spent 0.6 time studying and 0.4 at work so I could complete the retraining sooner and get on with full time in the school.

1992 saw me returning to full time work, having been retrained to teach computing, I thought it desirable I should begin to teach at least one class of it. Problem! Computing teachers were in over-abundance and Drama teachers did not exist in the school. I would have to teach Drama and Year 12 Drama at that! I had become a Drama teacher through practical experience, as a singer in Opera and a keen interest in acting. I had no academic training in the subject at all. That was required to teach Year 12!

---

[2] Port Lincoln High School is built on quite a sloping site. It was therefore a stiff climb from the Staff Room to the Drama Room.

I gritted my teeth, gave notice that I would exercise my "right of return" to the city for 1993 and got on with the task as best I could. By my own standards, I made a terrible job of it and they all passed. I only(sic) had one "incident" in the middle of the year when the stress levels had become too much from the *Group Production*[3] and I had been taken to hospital with a suspected heart attack. It wasn't. Only stress and MS.

We left the house we had only bought in 1987 which did not sell for another 12 months. Rental housing in Adelaide was necessary in the interim. It was not an enjoyable experience which saw us move house five times in fifteen months!

The next two- and a-bit years saw me at a highly regarded school in the city and my wife at the adjacent school. That made it easier for travelling in the morning. We were fortunate to be able to enrol our daughter in a nearby, highly regarded primary school. I taught computing and had the responsibility of managing the "old" network of computers. I also taught History in the junior years of the school. Eventually, I was confronted by the prospect of teaching Year 9 History in the second semester. I took the opportunity to resign. "Year 9's are Animals" was the title of an appropriately

---

[3] The Group Production was a major part of the assessment. A 'Moderator' came to visit the school and be a major part of assessing the students.

named play. Fortunately for me, I gained a position in a private school teaching computing and junior Geography for the second semester, to fill a hole left by a teacher who had left.

In January of 1996, we made a trip to New Zealand, travelling around in a motor home. That was most enjoyable and I was the only driver. No problems.

The years that followed became frustrating in the extreme. During these years my symptoms were mild with only occasional reminders I had a problem. I had taken a position with a telecommunications company where I would be paid only commission for sales I made. I tried my hardest yet could not make anything like a reasonable income. My beliefs about God had been changed to the polar opposite, without the desire to attend church.

I was not the man I used to be and my wife was having difficulty coping with that. When I became too impossible, she asked me to leave. I moved out after several tries. Perhaps the most memorable one was at Easter 2000. I began to vomit on Good Friday and continued to retch, after my stomach was empty, until the morning of Easter Monday. I had done much deep thinking in the half hour breaks between spasms. I had decided that I had to join a choir and also go to church.

I moved out soon after. During the time when I was not in the family home, I felt lost and incapable of making any sensible decision. I visited frequently to assist with transport of the children to and from school. It was during this period my mother came to her end at 92, from liver cancer, not old age. I spent one of the last weeks of her life with her at Paracombe, where she still lived, after 50 years there. It was where I had grown up from birth and others of the family reached adulthood. It was the Lewis family home. When it became too much for me to bear, my wife and daughter moved in to care for her for a few days until she was taken into a hospice for greater ease of care in the last few days of her life.

After she died, my wife invited me back into the family home where I lived for the next five years, through the forced sale of our home and moving into rental accommodation again.

My wife's mother decided she wanted to live with us and we were able to purchase a new home which had a facility that could be converted into a "Granny Flat". It was a very nice conversion for her and she lived in that, with us, for the next few years.

Eventually, when I became convinced I could not make a success out of commission only sales, I won a position in a different telecommunications company; in a call centre. Pay was by the week served. I worked as best I could in this position, until it became clear I was not meeting my sales targets. Several alternative roles were tried for me and I eventually had the responsibility for Occupational Health and Safety and the Environment. I saved the company my salary in waste paper in the first year in that role simply by explaining to the staff that they needed to set a "print area" in Excel[4] rather than print the whole sheet. That saved a huge number of pages going through the printer and being discarded in the waste paper bin.

A directive from senior management of the company meant that I could no longer hold this "unofficial" position and would have to resign. That left me in a position of having to rely on the Disability Support Pension as my only income.

In the meantime, I had moved out of the family home and into my own rental accommodation. I used public transport to get into and out of the city; parking fees were prohibitive. I did not enjoy standing all of the way on the bus either.

One noteworthy series of events occurred in my life outside of work. I was at a learning meeting with other blokes from the church I attended. I had driven myself there, not feeling too bad, and sat in a very comfortable armchair during the meeting.

---

[4] A Microsoft spreadsheet program which is almost ubiquitous.

When it became time to go, I could not stand up. At all! Body temperature had risen.

They were very good friends though. They managed to get me into one of their cars while another drove my car to where I was living. When I arrived, I still could not stand, let alone walk. Somehow, I got to the door where I sat on my office chair which one of my housemates had the brilliant idea of using to get to the toilet, my room and to bed. We realised that I could not look after myself so I rang for an ambulance and went to hospital until my temperature fell and I could walk again.

Soon after, I was most fortunate in that friends from the church offered me a place in a converted shed in their backyard. It proved very comfortable for a time.

Life continued until a new relationship caused me to seek a divorce and a move to Cairns.[5] I had it wrong! I had to find my own accommodation within a month during which she would go to Darwin to see her son and then I would be gone when she returned.

I found a new place to live, sharing a house with a

---

[5] Cairns is a city on the coast in far north Queensland. It has good access to the Great Barrier Reef and is the main city in FNQ. It provides many services to the area and was a really great place to live.

woman from the church for some time. We moved to a new place and took in a third member of the house; a young woman who was in need of a different place to live. Then I was invited to move in with another woman I had met. I had to help pay out the lease on the unit and my friends found a different place to live. (Reasonably so)

Eventually, in 2008, Queensland Housing offered me a brand-new apartment in a brand-new building. Amazing how all of the things I needed to set up my own place materialised. Even a barbeque, which I set up on the balcony of the first-floor apartment. It was not long before cooking a BBQ on the balcony required too much walking in and out for my deteriorating body. Living on my own proved a bit of a challenge. It required a different organisation for my meals so I could eat well enough and not be overcome by the energy required to prepare it. Breakfast became a smoothie, lunch a fresh avocado with lime juice and hot chilli and dinner became a selection from the stews, made in the slow cooker, and rice. The stews were made from a selection of the different meats I could buy from Rusty's Market, with the vegetables from there as well. The vegetables chosen were of a variety of colours, including turnips, swedes, tomatoes and capsicums as well as freshly washed leaves of spinach, Bok choy, kale or similar green leaf.

This worked well enough except I missed lunch a lot, being distracted by whatever else I might be doing such as games on the computer. As a result, I began to lose weight. It became a serious problem on one of my trips to the hospital when my body temperature became too high. With MS, it is often the case that temperature is a major factor in mobility and fatigue; too hot and loss of mobility occurs, to the point of being unable to stand or move my legs at any functional level.

One occasion, perhaps on my first visit to hospital in Cairns, is etched in my memory since I was so unable to do anything for myself. I felt really rotten for some reason, and had ordered and eaten a pizza. I stood, very shakily, and attempted to walk to the phone, while still maintaining one hand on my chair. Somehow, I fell backwards over the arm of my chair and then to the floor. I could not get up. I had to get to the phone to call an ambulance. Squirming can be one method of getting around. I made it to the phone and then the call. Then I had to get to the door to unlock it so they could get in.

I made it to the door by hauling myself on my back using the door frames to pull myself along. A few other firm handholds were used along the way. I unlocked the door just before the ambulance arrived. (I took steps to install a key safe outside the door the day I arrived home.)

On this occasion I learned a very useful lesson: ask

the Ambos to get me a urine bottle so I don't upset the triage nurse and wet myself at the same time. The neurogenic bladder knows no *wait* command. It just empties whenever it feels like it. And that is often as well. As a result, I had begun wearing pads inside my underpants. They were never very satisfactory but I did not think there was anything else, better. I got to be very adept at bladder emptying on the side of the road with discretion. It took another few years and a broken hip before I entered the world of catheters and, better, urodomes[6] and drain and leg bags.

It was not only my bladder that I had to deal with. MS also can make one's bowels neurogenic as well. That means that constipation was an ongoing problem with the occasional unexpected evacuation.

I lived, as I have explained elsewhere, with a number of different people in Cairns. I remember driving my car with my housemate and her adult son to the shops. It was a different shopping centre from our usual one. I felt the sudden urge and sought their assistance to find a toilet in a hurry. We could not and the inevitable occurred. I sat in it until we arrived home and I went through the necessary steps to clean myself up and also wash

---

[6] The urodome is similar to a condom, except that it has a "nozzle" into which a tube can be inserted. That tube leads to a bag, either worn on the leg or on the floor adjacent to the bed.

my clothes. I was exhausted that night and had to have their assistance to get my evening meal.

Another, really noteworthy experience I had in Cairns concerned my specialist neurologist. He had tried to convince me to go through the process of having an infusion of a steroid which had been used with some success with MS people. I eventually gave in and it was done in the week before the week before Easter on the Wednesday, Thursday and Friday. I was getting ready to drive, on my own, to Rockhampton, some 1100 Kms south and on the Tropic of Cancer. Easter was to be the time for the Queensland Eisteddfod, not just the North Queensland one.

My intention was to drive to Townsville and stay on Tuesday night with some friends who had moved there from Port Lincoln. The bulk of the journey would then be completed on Wednesday. That night would be spent in the hotel where I was intending to stay for the weekend. This would mean that I would be reasonably rested for a recitation of a poem for the first event of the Eisteddfod; "McArthur's Fart". I was given an Honourable Mention for that performance and then joined one of the Male Choir events next morning.

When it came time to get ready for a Mixed Choir event on Friday night, I found I could not move my left leg and therefore could not walk to the toilet or, by inference, onto the stage. It was disastrous! It meant hospital and a longer stay than expected because I was not allowed to drive myself when I was released. All of my friends from Cairns left on the Monday to get back in time for work the next day. I would not be ready for release until Tuesday. Therefore, I had to stay in hospital until someone could be flown down to Rockhampton and drive me home. What a to-do; the fare was about $800 on the regional airline and the flight bounced in Townsville and Mackay before it eventually reached Rockhampton. I am not sure but it might well have been cheaper to fly direct to Brisbane and then back to Rockhampton. The Choral Society paid for the fare which I thought was very generous. While I was sitting in the passenger seat on the way home, I used my mobile phone to make an appointment to see my doctor. I did so on arrival and he gave me permission to drive which I promptly did and dropped my friend off at his home and made it home myself. That whole week and a bit was quite an adventure.

The major result of these events was that I moved a motion of no confidence in the neurologist at the next meeting of the MS Support Group. I had seen the registrar rather than the neurologist at my next appointment who let slip that the infusion was contraindicated for people with secondary progressive MS. My notes would have had in them that I had been diagnosed with secondary progressive in 2004 by a neurologist in Adelaide, before I went to Cairns[7]. The motion was carried without any dissent and with many adding their experiences. I heard later that the situation changed so that anyone exhibiting symptoms was then seen by a visiting neurologist from Townsville. All treatments were also in his consultation.

While in Cairns I had joined a Lions Club and took an active role, serving as Secretary for two years and making a presentation at one meeting. I called it, "MS; a bitch of a complaint". It was very well received and, as a result, the President arranged for a significant donation towards setting up an exercise program for people with MS in the Cairns area. It was organised that we would use the PCYC, Police and Citizens Youth Club, gymnasium as a venue, and the physiotherapist who had been employed by the Queensland MS Society led the sessions.

At about the same time we hosted a visit from a member of the Brisbane staff of the Queensland MS Society with the proposal that we organise a MegaSwim[8] to raise funds for the Society. That occurred with significant enthusiasm by members of the Lions Club. It was a great success that year. The event had to be organised by the MS Society

---

[7] I had had my notes transferred for this very reason
[8] Copyright name which has meant several MS Societies around Australia now use a different name for the same event.

directly in the next year as there were significant problems with legal responsibility for the swimmers. We also had to call it something else for copyright reasons.

2013 was my final year in Cairns. After the Eisteddfod at Easter, I decided that I was lonely and also not safe on my own. I joined a Dating website. At the same time my soon-to-be wife was joined to that same site by a friend of hers. Her search parameters were set to within 50 Kms of Adelaide; my details appeared! In Cairns? 3000 Kms away!

We first spoke on July 17; for 6½ hours. I eventually said that it was time we went to bed. Whoops! That's not right. We laughed. Then agreed that we would talk again soon. We soon were using Skype to video talk from mid-morning until after dinner. It was possible for us to get some idea of the other's home. We really enjoyed our meals together and our life together on video call.

Eventually we agreed that it would be a good idea for Yvonne to come to Cairns and that was in September. She visited for two weeks and then returned to Adelaide. I then visited her for a fortnight in October. We thought it a good idea to take it to the next level and agreed to marry. It became obvious that I needed to leave Cairns in November. Somehow, I managed to get packed up and moved to Adelaide on November 14. Our marriage occurred on December 29 at Morphett

Vale.

During the next few years, my condition slowly deteriorated. There were occasions when continence issues raised their head. Severe fatigue was often the result and it was difficult on occasions to do what needed to be done. Falls often required the attendance of the ambulance and a stay in hospital.

In 2016 we were hosting our nieces. In an effort to make it possible for them to use a particular program on the computer, I attempted to plug some cords into the back of the TV. I fell over. I broke my hip. In fact, it was the neck of my femur. The neighbourhood knew about it! The ambulance was called again and a visit to hospital resulted. I did not return home for six months. I spent two weeks at Flinders Medical Centre, a number of weeks at the Repatriation Hospital and then 12 weeks at a rehabilitation place called Vita where I was rehabilitated.

I was assessed for Aged Care Residential Accommodation in early 2019. The information pack was overwhelming and I made no effort to complete the necessary paperwork. After a couple of months, I asked my daughter for help. It was clear that Yvonne could provide all of the individual parts of my help needs, but it would be too demanding to do all of it. Meanwhile, my daughter had completed the paperwork and applied for a place in several aged care homes. Eventually, I was offered a place at a home in Joslin, another suburb of Adelaide. This was a significant distance from Morphett Vale but it is probably the best home in Australia. I was surprised but most pleased and accepted the offer of a place immediately. I moved there on Maundy Thursday, Easter 2020, while the Pandemic raged around us and made life so different for many people.

As I reflect on my life with MS, the visions that I had for my life have had to be drastically changed. There have been occasions when it was becoming too difficult, so giving up was most appealing. That way was not for me; at least not yet. The rubber bands which I had used for resistance training for my upper body have been a part of daily life for years. The addition of a Thera cycle meant that I had something for my legs and possibly my heart when I used it for my arms. It proved too difficult to lift off the floor and use it with my arms as well as my legs. Providing a place where this could be done was the problem, so it did not happen. The philanthropic generosity of the real estate investing club, of which my son was a member, was therefore not so beneficial as it might have been in slowing the progress of the complaint in me. It needs to be remembered that every person with MS has a different experience with it. I count myself most fortunate to have had a much slower progression than most. Some have suggested that it is the determination I have displayed and the physical exercise regime I have followed which has been the reason for the slow progression. That may be the case. That is for others to contemplate. I just get on with making my life as good as I can in the best circumstances I can find.

Of significance during all of this is my developing Christian thinking and faith. It has coloured, or maybe directed much of my thinking. It has become an increasing part of my life. Of particular importance is my strong belief that the Bible has much advice which helps with life decisions.

My thoughts on attitudes and emotional state are expressed elsewhere, later in the book. Suffice it to say here, that the only way to look at life is up. And that is a choice to be made all the time. I have made major mistakes, largely as a result of the confusion and self-doubt which have stemmed from MS. I could really beat myself up over them. There is no point in doing that. I do other things instead, including writing this book.

I am most fortunate in so many ways; my first wife and her support before our divorce, my siblings and my children as well as the friends I have made along the way, have all been an invaluable support. Then to be here, where everything is done and nearly everything provided. Fortunate beyond belief. There is only one thing I could see as being an improvement. I will hang on to that and it will keep me going to try to be here when it happens.

Give it a go, mate. What is success to you?

How many people will attend your funeral because they really want to say goodbye or pay their respects on a purely personal level? I reflect on my father's funeral here, for a moment. He died suddenly at the age of seventy when I was about to turn twenty-five. He and Mum had ten children and the numbers at his funeral were incomprehensible to me at the time. I thought that he had not made any major or significant marks in the world. He had spent all of my life as an orchard labourer; working for someone else. He had only reached Grade 7 at school. He was my Dad, nothing special, or so I thought. Yet there were at least 2 kilometres of cars in his funeral procession! There was clearly something else present here. It could only be the way he approached life and any problems that arose in his vicinity.

How are you going to judge your life as being a success? Is it appropriate even to consider judging yourself anyway? Put yourself in the position of being seventy-five years of age. When you look back on your life so far, has it been what you think you would like it to have been? What are your ambitions, then? These are profoundly important questions we all would do well to ask as we get to know our changing selves. Sometimes the answers are not what we really like. The good news is, it's never too late to make changes so the answers are better. This is certainly my hope anyway as I embark on making the changes to what I want to be as compared with what I am, now. I have really stuffed up along the way, particularly in my relationships.

And by the way, a very wise person said once, "Life is what happens when you are busy making other plans."[9]

It is only ourselves who are responsible for what we do and therefore it is only us who can judge the degree of success we are achieving or have achieved. If we want to be independent thinkers and informed opinion holders, we need to take responsibility for all that we do and say, in all aspects of our lives. The principle of accepting responsibility includes accepting the successes as well as the less than successful. It may also include acknowledging the contribution of many others in the success. It would be a better society to live in if those who have chosen to be a part of the political process held and practiced this axiom; of being transparently responsible. It certainly has application in our relationships, our finances, our employment and in our families in the way we bring up our children. One might say that accepting responsibility is a fundamental principle of living in a democracy and that for the democracy to thrive,

---

[9] John Lennon

that principle must have a major acceptance throughout the community.

Some people may switch off as soon as they read these words. I ask that my readers bear with me for a moment since they provide the tools we need to understand and even participate in the discussion. They all relate to KNOWING. René Descartes used as the basis for his philosophical method, the phrase, "I doubt, therefore I think, therefore I am"[10]. For most of us it is our *faith* that determines what we *believe* to be *true* and therefore *know*. It is important for each of us to seek and find our own truths about all of what is important or not. That search is what shapes our lives as we develop beliefs about the world in which we live and ourselves.

I spent considerable time and money attending self-help seminars run by the current "wise man" or "guru". Then I started to read Matthew in the New Testament and was amazed that it was all there. Perhaps the words were not quite the same. Without exception, everything I heard from the "gurus" was to be found in the Gospels or elsewhere in the Bible. Even if you don't want to be a Christian, a follower of Christ, you can save yourself a lot of money by consulting the Bible through one of the

---

[10] *Cogito ergo sum* is the Latin abbreviated form of what Descartes wrote. See the entry in Wikipedia for a more detailed discussion.

numerous search engines found on the web for this very purpose. Everything is in it and all that is in this book can be found there in some form. It even provides a manual for healing, although I do not advocate not consulting your doctor. For most of us, the best way for managing illness, even when it is described as incurable, is to follow medical advice.

To begin, I outline a few axioms or measures I have learned about living successfully, providing biblical references. Since I also consider that God wants me to be the greatest success in all ways that I can be, it becomes part of my belief that God's Word is a wonderful source of guidance as well.

Money

I share elsewhere that I spent most of my life believing that I never had enough money. The Bible gives a clear idea as to how to ensure that there is always enough, even if it might seem it would be better if there were more. There can be. I have been dependent on the pension provided by the Government to people living with a disability for my whole income for quite a few years. In the Bible there is discussion of tithing, giving 10% of one's income to God, being the source of greater income. In my case, I give money to the church I attend and to a charity I have chosen to support. Other needy causes arise from time to time and they sometimes get my support as well. It does not seem to make sense to give income away to increase it, yet it works!

People in business understand that they make an investment so they can gain a return in reward for their service, innovation, research or whatever. Tithing is a similar concept, although it is often misunderstood as being like a tax. The difference is that one tithes for the purpose of returning to God, the universe or whatever is the motivating factor for the individual, a part of what has been received. The quantity of one's income is usually dependent on a variety of factors, only some of which are in the control of the individual. In another sense then, tithing could be seen as paying back for the provision of those factors. I count myself as "well off" since I have that security provided by my government. Others who have a much greater income than I are dissatisfied with it and go through life, miserable, because they do not celebrate what they have; like I did until I learned otherwise. Life becomes so much better if one celebrates the wealth one has rather than bemoaning that others have more. That does not necessarily mean they do not have enough.

If one wants more, the simple measure to achieve that is to give more. For example, Ephesians chapter 6 verse 8 in one translation says, "'because you know that the Lord will reward each one for whatever good they do, whether they are slave or free.[11]' It may not be that one gives more money. There are many other things that can be given away that may return more wealth. The most important point here is that one celebrates whatever one has and is prepared to share it with others. The ways in which one can give more are endless.

I admit that it took me a while to accept fully that this really did work. A number of instances led me to believe that I would always have enough. It has made for a much less stressful life knowing that all expenses for those things that are necessary will be met by funds that will be available when the time is right. Elsewhere there are more illustrations of how it might work.

Give more and stress less!

Self Talk

Another way in which we can make our lives better is to follow the advice given in the truism, "the stories we tell ourselves are the ones that come true". A number of the teachers I went to advised the use of affirmations. I discovered "The tongue has the power of life and death, and those who love it will eat its fruit."[12]. It seems that the advice was before me all along. I just did not recognise it for what it is. Perhaps it was necessary for me to hear the numerous teachers and the suggestion that

---

[11] NIV Ephesians 6:8
[12] NIV Proverbs 18:21

affirmations, or the tongue, had such power. More about affirmations shortly.

The tongue is so important in making our lives successful. It needs to be guarded as well so it does not create confusion in the subconscious. Judging others or oneself is one sure way in which to confuse the subconscious. I suggest and explain elsewhere that there are two words that our vocabulary would be better off without: they are "should" and "ought". They imply judgement of another or oneself. Easy substitutions are "could" and "might". Hence, instead of saying, "I should do more to encourage my kids", it becomes "I could do more. . . .". Another example is, "I ought to be better at helping around the house", becomes, "I might be a better husband if I accepted my share of the household tasks". Judging ourselves might be worse than judging others but more about judgement later.

Affirmations

The repetition of statements as if they are true is suggested as a way of achieving goals. It certainly works, even in the negative sense that when we say something, often it becomes true when we do not really want that at all. One of the best examples is that which deals with memory. For example, when we forget a person's name and we then say aloud or even to ourselves, "I always forget peoples' names", it reinforces the forgetfulness that we want to be better. In such a case, the thought might be caught and changed to, "I remember names a lot of the time'. It is still true and leads to a more successful memory of names rather than the forgetfulness we often find embarrassing. It would be beneficial if that affirmation were repeated several times whenever a person's name is sought from memory or it seems to have been forgotten. It might also be useful if we found a method to improve our memory of names. One such is to use the name several times in conversation, immediately.

Similarly, any situation that we seek to change or any set of behaviours we want to improve upon can be the basis for creating affirmations. It is important that they be **stated in the positive** and that they be true in some regard at least. I must emphasise that last sentence. Affirmations are better if they are in a positive statement and cannot be dismissed as a lie. Another way of putting it is, **'the stories we tell ourselves are the ones that come true'**.

The Bible does not seem to provide any simple and direct statement about affirmations and I take a risk stating that, as someone will disagree immediately and with certainty. Of relevance here are a couple of references: The Proverbs text quoted earlier[13] is a good start. Also, Romans 12:2 "Do not conform to the pattern of this world but be transformed by the renewing of your mind.[14]" Our ability to make changes to ourselves is in our own hands. Of significance here as well as the acceptance of responsibility is Hebrews 12: 11 "For the time being no discipline brings joy, but seems grievous and painful; but afterwards it yields a peaceable fruit of righteousness to those who have been trained by it...[15]" If we choose to catch those thoughts that are unhelpful and replace them with something that is, then we are exercising self-discipline and the result will be much greater success in achieving what we want. Perhaps most important and applying everywhere is Matthew 4:4 " ... live ... by every word that proceeds from the mouth of God[16]." The Bible is considered by many to be the word inspired by God so it is an excellent guide for all our behaviour if we want to be successful.

Judgement

The tongue is such a powerful tool that it can sometimes be misused. It is good to be able to

---

[13] Proverbs 18:21 "Words kill, words give life; they're either poison or fruit—you choose." *The Message*
[14] NIV
[15] NIV
[16] New King James Version

throw over our shoulder anything that might be said by another about us to our face or is something we hear unwittingly. The Bible has some advice to give here. 'Also, do not take seriously all words which are spoken, so that you will not hear your servant cursing you. For you also have realised that you likewise have many times cursed others.'[17] Hang on to that advice. It has been a part of my experience that an inability to throw some overheard curses over my shoulder led to a serious loss of self-confidence. I was unable to work for several months as a result. You are good at your job if you want to be, so let no-one suggest otherwise!

Making judgements about others is very self-destructive behaviour. Luke 6:41-42 is quite clear (sic): "Why do you look at the speck in your brother's eye, but fail to notice the plank in your own eye? How can you say, 'Brother, let me take the speck out of your eye,' while you yourself fail to see the beam in your own eye? You hypocrite, first take the plank out of your own eye, and then you will see clearly to remove the speck from your brother's eye."[18] Even clearer is Matthew 7:1-2 "1 **Do not judge, or you too will be judged. For in the same way you judge others, you will be judged, and with the measure you use, it will be measured to you."**[19] So when you

---

[17] NIV Ecclesiastes 7: 21-22
[18] NIV Luke 6:41-42
[19] NIV Matthew 7:1-2

are driving and you see another driver do something less than desirable, catch yourself when you are about to yell out the window that he is somehow less than he might be or words to that effect and remember that he might be someone who has much that can be described as admirable in his character. He might also meet you later in the day and you discover that he is not anything like that being you so graphically described but a really nice and influential person that you might want to impress! Whoops!

Rest

One frequent mistaken belief is that one needs to put in incredibly lengthy hours if the returns are to follow. I thought I was doing the right thing when I sought to continue working into my break time when I first started a new job in a call centre. It was pointed out quite forcefully that my overall productivity required me to take the breaks that had been set down and that in future I would take the breaks for the benefit of the company! Figures were provided that showed the wisdom of this in the long run. Hence the advice that Jesus gave his disciples is valid for us as well. 'Come aside by yourselves...and rest a while.'[20]

In these periods of rest that we take, it gives us the opportunity to allow our minds to visit many different places. More about that elsewhere, perhaps. We can use them for prayer, meditation, where we allow God to be

---

[20] NIV Mark 6:31

heard, or just to wander into places that it wants to go. A degree of caution needs to be exercised here in that we always need to ensure that the self-talk that occurs is of benefit. It has a tendency to go places that are not helpful. One such is to revisit that occasion when we were mistreated, insulted or even physically attacked in some way.

Forgiveness

One of the most important understandings that I have gained is that forgiveness is for **my** benefit, not for the person who aggrieved me. While I maintain that feeling of justified hurt, I keep myself in that place where it happened; that hurt lives on. To escape from and be healed is the goal. Forgiveness does that in a heartbeat. It may feel very difficult to forgive because the hurt was so grave. However, it is possible to find a small bit of forgiveness somewhere and the healing begins. It is worth repeating.

I forgive for my benefit, not for the other person's.

The Amplified Bible gives a very useful explanation of why forgiveness is such a valuable decision: "But if you do not forgive others [nurturing your hurt and anger with the result that it interferes with your relationship with God], then your Father will not forgive your trespasses."[21] It is worth considering this a little longer. The bracketed part, "nurturing your hurt and anger . . . "interferes with the success you might feel in your life as well as your relationship with God, if that is important to you.

There are many other references in the Bible that deal with forgiveness. Jesus discussed and used it on many occasions. It was an important part of His healing. It can be most valuable to us in the same way.

There are, of course, those who cannot get out of that place of wallowing in the aggrievement, that justified sense of hurt, that "poor me" place that seems so justified. It might be justified and it will certainly ensure a most unhappy life. Stay there if that is what you want!

Friendship

I could write thousands of words on this and still not capture what it means to be a friend. What is important is that we all have friends, or just a friend, and that they may change from time to time. There is an adage about friends: they are for a reason, a season or a lifetime. It is almost impossible to live without friends. We share our lives with our friends.

---

[21] Matthew 6:15 (AMP)

What seems to me most important about friendship is the openness and honesty that are at the core of that relationship. If we put that another way it means that love has a most important role to play. Obviously, physical intimacy between lovers is different from the love between friends.

As soon as the word love is mentioned, another limitless discussion is opened. That is not part of my musings that I can write about. Part of my musings on the subject is dealt with in the chapter, **"Do you want more?"** The nature of the relationship between friends is much beyond anything that I can encapsulate in any written diatribe; it's simply too vast and well beyond my analytical ability here.

Perhaps I can make a little suggestion; that the Bible has extensive texts about friendship and love that seem to me to be central issues to all our lives[22].

Generosity

The axiom, "if you want more, you need to give more", is something we can all take to heart. It seems counter-intuitive yet it works. The principle of tithing is a small part of this idea. Elsewhere I

---

[22] Yes, I chickened out of trying to provide any analysis of these critically important issues that form such a crucial role in our lives. Please forgive me. My thoughts on the subjects are too vast to analyse.

said that some see the tithe as a tax. I pointed out it is more like an investment. The same principle applies here when we give all we have and receive so much more in return. It must be pointed out that giving and receiving are not confined to the material. What we give and receive can be in the spiritual, emotional and temporal areas as a minimum. When we examine the principle closely, it begins to make sense. In the material realm, investing wisely gives greater returns. The more that is invested, the greater is the return. When you give of your time to valuable enterprise, for example, a child, the returns are immeasurable without anything of the material involved in the immediate time frame. It may also be the case that investing time into a business venture will see it return significant value. The nature of the giving does not necessarily see a return in the same area. The simple axiom stated at the beginning of this discussion holds true in some way, regardless of the nature of the generosity or the return. The act of giving generously is in itself its own reward. We can feel good about the assistance we might have provided if that is the nature of the generous act. It must be pointed out that one is not generous because it will create more for us. That corrupts the generosity and spoils the return. The spirit of generosity must always be without thought of reward. It will come in ways that are frequently surprising.

The Ego: its value and its treachery

It seems there may be some differing interpretations of the word "ego". Many assume it to mean something similar to excess pride or self-absorption. An alternative understanding is that the Ego is a necessary part of all our psyches and is the source of most of our achievements. As part of the training to become a Journey[23] Practitioner, I learned about the Ego and the way it affects us all in ways of which we are totally unaware. I make no claim to be any sort of expert on the Ego other than that it is a major shaper of what choices we make and actions we take, often unconsciously. I point readers in the direction of the Enneagram[24] and the Journey because they provide an understanding well beyond anything I can communicate.

For those who see the Ego as referring to excessive pride, the Bible has many passages that advise most

---

[23] The Journey is a process-based tool for healing in many aspects of life. Visit the website for a more complete outline of its benefits and purpose. It was created by Brandon Bays and is now a worldwide organisation. It includes a tool that is useful in alerting us to the subconscious motivations for action that may lead us into difficulties: the Ego. Part of that is enabling us to make more objective decisions rather than to be led by our Ego.

[24] The Enneagram has its origins in ancient times and has been developed further in the twentieth Century as a tool for personality typing. It is very useful in that it provides tools that can be used to ensure well-founded actions are taken in this world rather than those that might be less helpful.

strongly against having that attitude to oneself and life. In fact, one of the fundamental teachings of Christ is to live our lives humbly. That does not mean that we must be poor; only that we show gratitude for what we have and seek to be generous with it. That way we will gain most benefit in ways beyond the material. We can use the gifts we have been given to be very successful in any way we choose. That will be a significant reward in itself.

The treachery of the Ego lies in both meanings. We can make decisions or choose to act in ways that are from pride. The old axiom of "pride coming before a fall" is found in Old Testament biblical texts as well in the culture of the ancient Greeks[25]. It is also the case that the Ego can be the basis for the type of decisions for actions we have made. The Enneagram gives a much better explanation of how this works and can become the basis for becoming aware of and gaining conscious control, rather than unconscious, of the action and word choices we make. It is well worth pursuing the awareness of the type of personality each of us are so that we can become conscious of what it is that drives us.

---

[25] Many of the ancient Greek tragedies deal with this theme. There is a suggestion that the drama festivals of ancient Greece were beneficial in social development as well as for entertainment. The notions of *hubris, nemesis* and the inevitable *catharsis* could be applied to the central character as well as for the audience.

It is important to remember that there are no better types of personality; only different. I would advise against making any judgements of a person on the basis of what type you think they might be. We would mislead ourselves most certainly if we were to do that. It is almost impossible for one individual to decide what another is with any certainty. That judgement can best be made by the individual and only them.

It is worth exploring the Bible further to see what it has to say about thoughts and becoming conscious of the motivations we have. I will leave that to the reader.

Goal setting

The use of goal setting is another tool for achieving more of what you want from life. Habakkuk 2:2-4[26] provides a very clear instruction about this technique. It permeates the business community as a technique for being more successful, getting more, better sales results or more income etc. It can work well although framing the affirmation is fraught; its nature can be given as the reason for not achieving the results expected just as much for explaining the success achieved. I am no expert and

---

[26] 2 And the Lord answered me:
"Write the vision; make it plain on tablets, so he may run who reads it. 3 For still the vision awaits its appointed time; it hastens to the end—it will not lie. If it seems slow, wait for it; it will surely come; it will not delay."

I suggest getting guidance elsewhere. I do know that one principle is that the affirmation needs to be framed in the positive for it to have any chance of success. Additional features I have been taught are that it also needs to be specific and detailed.

Business

I have decided that I am not a business man; it proves what I have been saying about self-talk and affirmations. I have tried to make a success of business and have failed. I am too old, in my own opinion, now to begin again in an effort to make a success of it. Rapid fatigue from Multiple Sclerosis might have something to do with it as well. My affirmations are that it is not a possibility for me. I do encourage others close to me though, especially when they are feeling a bit doubtful of their path. I don't try and shove the Bible at them since that would be counterproductive. Proverbs 3:6 gives some very good advice here though. That and the following verses provide guidance that any business coach might be proud of or even choose to pass on.

Self discipline

Teaching yourself is always difficult. I certainly have found it so. It is so easy to give in to the easy way rather than the way which leads to much greater success and sooner and better, even more satisfying. A number of passages from the Bible give good guidance here. And they are free to you whenever you want to go there and look. 'For the time being no discipline brings joy, and (discipline) seems grievous and painful; but afterwards it yields a peaceable fruit of righteousness to those who have been trained by it...'[27] 'Lead me, O Lord, in Your righteousness because of my enemies—make straight Your way before me.' (Psalm 5:8 NIV) 'Guide me in Your truth and teach me, for You are God my Saviour, and my hope is in You all day long.' (Psalm 25:5 NIV) 'Teach me Your way, Lord; lead me in a straight path.' (Psalm 27:11 NIV) 'Teach me to do Your will, for You are my God; may Your good Spirit lead me on level ground.' (Psalm 143:10 NIV) The search engines of the internet provide a very easy manner of finding out what the Bible has to say about anything.

While I have focussed here on suggesting ways you can be "successful", it really is your decision and your description of what you want your success to look like. I have laid out my set of values and attitudes that drive the choices made and the beliefs about the life I choose to live. I consider myself a beginner in being the man I could be. All of us need to remember that life has no rehearsal. It is always the opening night. Perhaps it might even be helpful to think along those lines; the celebratory nature of the occasion being applied to every moment of our

---

[27] Hebrews 12:11

lives. It is almost imperative to sound the note of caution that our present choices affect our future in ways we cannot understand: that the celebrations need to be of a non-destructive nature. That is why it has become easier and easier to live as a child of God, seeking to follow the life which God has provided for me. At least that way there is the security of knowing that it really will be "alright on the night", in theatre parlance.

I strongly suggest you take a different approach from what I have done. The easy way almost always ends up leading you somewhere else. The road to success is one of self-discipline. "Don't look for shortcuts to God. The market is flooded with sure-fire, easy-going formulas for a successful life that can be practiced in your spare time. Don't fall for that stuff, even though crowds of people do. The way to life—to God!—is vigorous and requires total attention."[28] I am getting better at living a productive and joyful life as I get older. It's taken me long enough and I am still a beginner. Of course, you might want to go somewhere else!

---

[28] **The Message**, Eugene H. Peterson Matthew 7:13-14

And this is why

"Any system carries the seeds of its own destruction".

"Democracy carries the seeds of its own destruction as well as the means to self-perpetuate".

Karl Marx used the principle when he claimed, "capitalism contains the seeds of its own destruction". I have added the idea that it can also perpetuate itself to complete the picture and to discredit Marx's additional notion that its destruction was inevitable[29]. We can have a society that is continually changing within the boundaries of shared foundational principles that serve all people to the best benefit for all. It is the responsibility of all of its citizens to make sure the changes we allow are supportive of the best benefit of all our citizens, not just ourselves or the few who are more influential or wealthy than others.

Of primary interest here is the system of government we often refer to as DEMOCRACY. It is not just any system of democracy that is our focus but it is that system which has evolved mainly in Western Europe. It is claimed by some

---

[29] I am sure there have been many others before me who have seen this truth. I have not seen it expressed before.

political leaders that their version is "true" democracy. That view is often debated with logic and heat. Some of the distinguishing features that are the focus here are:

The people are the source of all legitimacy of the government in some significant way, usually through the free right to elect those who represent them;

* The principle of universal suffrage: we all get a vote if we are old enough;
* The system contains the legal means by which government is changed; that is, through elections.
* The Constitution has established independent means for counting the votes so they are a real reflection of diverse views within the electorate.
* Elections are held periodically and all may seek election without fear of physical or other forms of abuse.
* The legal system is above all else and is based on a Constitution setting out how the system works and guaranteeing certain rights and responsibilities.
* The system of government contains at least Legislative, Judicial and Executive

components, all of which are bound by the Constitution in what they can and cannot do and how they relate to the other components.

Implicit in this system is the principle that everyone gets a fair chance at success and those who find they are unable to look after themselves are provided for, at least in the short term. Also implied is that there are opportunities for people to hold different opinions and belief systems, provided they do not threaten the rights of others in the community. Fundamentally, everyone is equal before the LAW.

People often look back at the system of ancient Athens and describe it as a Democracy. I do not dispute that. It was a city-state where the population was considerably smaller than the nation states that exist today and the social system was founded on slavery, a very undemocratic system indeed. While the idea of democracy had a presence there, it was not applied to all people, regardless of social standing.

One could write at great length about what makes a democracy. My focus here is in two areas: the tolerance of a range of beliefs and attitudes and the role of the legal system as part of the whole. This is outlined very well in the Easter Message presented by British PM David

Cameron in 2016[30]. It is fascinating to consider the notion that Jesus Christ was an egalitarian, the basis of democracy: humility was a feature of His life and he made a point of spending His time with the lower ranked people on the ladder of social standing. A reading of the Gospels or first four books of the New Testament of The Bible make that very plain.

Democracies in the twenty first century have their origins in the Judaeo-Christian traditions and sets of values. It is a truism that all democracies that do exist have developed within that tradition or have been heavily influenced by it, perhaps through a colonial background. Because most of the population have some attachment in thought if not faith to that religious background, then they have been strongly influenced by it and have accepted the practice of the religion existing in their society. The citizenry may hold a range of beliefs, some claiming no belief at all. There is a general awareness that we all must accept that there are differences and that there are only negative outcomes if we do not do so. As a result, the principle of *Tolerance* has become a value in our society and people can use "intolerant" as a

---

[30] https://www.gov.uk/government/news/easter-2016-david-camerons-message

negative label in any propaganda or discussion. As a result, some people push the boundaries of accepted beliefs, behaviours and values. The underlying principle to which the society needs to adhere, and generally does, is that the rights of individuals should not be affected to the detriment of the wellbeing of the whole population. The contrary notion is that we need to avoid the tyranny of the majority. It is always finding the point of balance between the two maxims.

The history of democracies has been littered with major struggles, sometimes revolutionary, where the aim has been to improve the rights of those who are seen as being lower in status. In the United Kingdom it was the Magna Carta and a number of other insurrections and the struggles to create a unity of England, Scotland, Wales and Ireland. In France the number of revolutions that succeeded in bringing about such change makes for fascinating reading and is the source of many creations in the Arts[31]. The point here is that these nations have had to fight

---

[31] A prime example here is *Les Misérables,* set during one of the many revolutions in France and the events leading to it. Victor Hugo wrote a huge novel and discussed important democratic principles of opportunities for all and the responsibility we share in providing for that. The popular musical based on the book provides some insight into the issues raised by the original novel. Another example that springs to mind is the novel, "The Scarlet Pimpernel".

to achieve the egalitarian and tolerant societies they currently enjoy, partly because they have also suffered wars over the right to hold the particular version of Christian belief which is dominant there.

The value of the life of an individual, one of God's children, has been a key motivating factor in the resolution of all the conflicts that have occurred. At the root of this tolerant, egalitarian and just society is the notion of humanity found in Genesis Chapter 1 verse 27: "So God created man in his own image, in the image of God he created him; male and female he created them."[32] Even more, if we look at the life of the man upon whom the Christian religion is based, we find that he had quite humble beginnings. He spent his time mainly with ordinary people, many of whom came from what was considered lower social groups; tax collectors, prostitutes and even a Samaritan woman (someone from a different ethnic group that were considered inferior by the Jews). He was an egalitarian to the core who also healed a Centurion's child (a Roman, worse as he was from the external rulers). Social or political station was of no significance to him. Nor was gender. Many women had significant roles in his life and he

---

[32] New King James Version

always treated them as equals without even thinking too much about it. He was more than tolerant as he taught that Love of fellow humans was an essential part of being a human in society.

With the foundation of the set of beliefs about the nature of the Deity and God's son, the development of a political system which holds human life to be sacrosanct and that all people are given equality in the best way that can be achieved for the benefit of all, it is not surprising that the Judaeo-Christian ethic has produced the liberal democracies which exist today. Tolerance is valued very highly so all can live together in a peaceful and non-violent society.

Critical to the political system which has developed is the establishment in law of the egalitarian principles that have been discussed. Those principles mean nothing without the foundation of the rule of law and that all people should be considered in the same way by it.

The Roman *Pax Romana* is the foundation for the idea that Law must prevail over all; that any conflict must be settled through the Law rather than through any other means as those other means are likely to produce further conflict, often of a violent and perhaps deadly nature. The *Pax Romana* really only applied to Roman citizens so all of the other peoples had no standing in that Law and there was therefore significant injustice. Jesus influenced major changes to the notion of the rule of Law with his crucifixion bringing God's Grace to all people, regardless of ethnicity or status. His influence was significantly enhanced when the Roman Empire embraced the Christian religion to the exclusion of others. It is worth noting here that the embrace of the Christian religion by the Romans was also a major factor in its corruption since, pragmatically, it had to allow for a huge range of different belief systems and still allow the label Christian.

The Roman concept of the rule of law took a submersion for quite a few years in Europe as a variety of different despotic rulers had their way in the development of the idea of nation states instead of kingdoms and empires. (This in no way is meant to suggest that nation states were an inevitable outcome of what we call mediaeval times and does make a huge leap over centuries and generations.) Nonetheless, in Britain at least, the notion of justice for all did rear its head in the Magna Carta. With the additional influences which were part of the Renaissance, old notions surfaced again and the rule of law became a catch cry for people in Europe. With that idea was the notion of Justice for all people.

It only (sic) took a few centuries to gain a firm foothold as more and more people were included in the definition of ALL.

Along with the development of the notion of *Justice* for all and the rule of Law was the means by which laws could be made; the development of the various legislatures and the means by which those Assemblies, Parliaments or whatever name was chosen were elected. The most common method was through representation; the idea that the population would elect a Representative who best showed their general views or that they thought would assist in making laws which suited them.

To draw a few strands together: Democracy is supposed to be "rule by the people". Practically that has led to the concept of representational rule. This is supposed to mean Justice for all in a society that largely follows the rule of law. Now throw in the idea that "all systems contain the seeds of their own destruction" and "Power corrupts, absolute power corrupts absolutely"[33], and we consider what seems to be developing. If we consider that representational democracy is becoming less representational in that the occupations of elected representatives are not a

---

[33] Sir John Dalberg-Acton, 8th Baronet. Used the phrase, " Power tends to corrupt, and absolute power corrupts absolutely. . . ."

reflection of the occupations of the community at large[34], then there is a possible problem. Throw in the dislike of politicians in general because "they only want to know you when its election time", whether that really be true or not, and the result is that our representatives are representing us less and less; they are becoming less and less accessible to us as individuals because they are "protected" by staff whose job it is to prevent all and sundry from making the life of the representative impossibly busy.

What is of major concern is that the trades and unskilled workers are not being represented; unless one considers their university graduate lawyer former Union leaders are their representatives. It would be most unlikely today that the Prime Minister has a background in the mines as did Andrew Fisher and Joseph Cook. The separation of representative from elector in prior occupation is at least in part the root of that separation. The matter of gender is an additional related issue that has led to the view that our representative democracies are not very representative of the society at large. The key

---

[34] "Who Sits in Parliament", Dr Robyn Hollander, Refereed paper presented to the Australasian Political Studies Association Conference University of Tasmania, Hobart, 29 September – 1 October 2003

response to this is that elected representatives are elected every few years, be it three or four, depending on the place. If they are serious about being re-elected, they must have convinced enough of the electorate that they have been good representatives of the local area. This has been shown to be possible even in a situation where the party affiliations have taken on a greater importance than the representative's efforts and abilities. Nonetheless, it follows that the representative must have the ability to communicate if they are to carry out the job effectively. It would appear that it is the lawyers who are becoming more influential in the law-making role because of that.

That raises another issue. Lawyers have often seen themselves as an essential part of the processes of the law because they are the only ones who have been trained in the special language used. This could easily be seen as the development of a separate, superior group, separated from the rest of the society, and thus anti-democratic. Additionally, there might be a concern that lawyers, as the elected representatives, are having more influence over the making of the law as well as the special role in its application. There is already much truth in the advice that only a fool represents himself in court. That is the domain of those trained in the law; barristers, various counsels, judges and magistrates.

We find that governments also need to employ lawyers in a variety of roles that can lead to conflicts of interest. This is where the "power corrupts" adage begins to take on a more sinister possibility: when a person uses his or her special position to have undue influence over the processes that are in place. All people, everywhere, need to be very careful and watchful that this corruption does not take place, else our whole system becomes at risk of descending into the lawless state which almost all would seek to prevent, even the perpetrators of that corruption. After all, the degree of their success is dependent on the rest of us following the law.

The Museum of Australian Democracy[35] website provides much discussion about democracy and is worth exploring if one wants to gain a greater understanding of democracies in general.

The discussion here seeks only to inform people about the necessities of observing the values of a liberal democracy if it is to continue to meet the needs of the population of the nation state. It is an emphasis on those values which underpin

---

[35] https://www.moadoph.gov.au/democracy/#

our society so that there is a "fair go" for all of our citizens and that we can ensure we all live in peace, prosperity and security. We also need to recognise that there are people in other countries who would seek the same ends but are currently denied them for a host of reasons. We are, after all, global as well as national citizens. An important function of our state is to ensure that it perpetuates itself in tune with the desires of its citizens. A look back at the values found in the Judaeo-Christian tradition is valuable for us all. They are so helpful as the basis for living a highly productive and valuable life for oneself as much as for the community at large. It is clear there is a need for us all to be aware of those values and the importance they have for our society.

Some Christians would argue that the best system of government is a theocracy or "rule by God". That sounds like it would be terrific except for the example of John Calvin in Geneva. He claimed to have a special relationship with God and therefore a monopoly on what God wanted. It was much more like an autocracy since he dictated what was right and wrong and was corrupted by that power as he committed what can only be described as unchristian acts. The most notorious of these was his burning of Michael Servetus for his "heretical beliefs".

Power corrupts, absolute power corrupts absolutely is a maxim we need to keep near to prevent corruption in government and therefore the criminal inequity which is the result.

But there is more to the system of government that calls for further discussion in this chapter about having a better government. And don't we deserve it?

Earlier I outlined some of the features of "Western Democracy" and included that systems included the sections of Legislative, Judicial and Executive. In reality, all political systems include these three functions in some form or another. It is my strong opinion that the executive should never be elected directly by the people. In this system, far too much money is spent on getting elected to the position. To make it clear, what I am really suggesting is that the system in the USA is flawed. The ideal of "separation of powers" seems good but has difficulties in the effective operation of a government.

Let's get down to brass tacks. The Founding Fathers in the USA believed that George III (the British Monarch or King at the time) was a tyrant. They sought to make it impossible for such to rear its ugly head in their system of government. What they got right is that a tyrant could not last if a mistake was made and one was elected. The problem here is that they came to believe their own propaganda; George III was not a tyrant since he was already restricted by the necessity to include the Parliament in any action taken.

The system they devised works pretty well most of the time. Unfortunately, there are some aspects which seem not to. Those occasions occur when there is significant conflict between the President (Head of State; Executive) and the controlling, or majority, representatives in one or both of the chambers of the Legislature. If that happens, there can be a major road block in getting the business of government done; of getting anything done. In this system, there are three hurdles that even most desirable changes have to jump; President, Senate and Congress (Executive and Upper House and Lower House of the Legislature). It is sometimes difficult, nay impossible, to get it through. The difficulty is the ideological beliefs of those holding the majority or the office. It could also be because the form of the measure is not of adequate similarity to the one suggested by one section. Essentially, the problem lies in that there is not a necessarily strong enough link between the authors of the laws and those who put them into effect.

What I believe to be the major weakness in this system is not described above. Rather, it is the way the Executive is created. Huge sums are spent on being pre-selected by a major political party and who knows what deals are made with donors to the cause. Once that is achieved, the next step is the campaign itself. The costs of the campaign are huge and are of no real benefit to the community as a whole. The result is that only the wealthy become the President or Chief Executive and huge sums are spent on the election of an additional position of the system of government. It is wasteful and also lends itself to the corruption of the system by the backroom "deals" done along the way. The elected become the elite and non-representative of their electors in a most undemocratic manner.

One might add that there has been a major challenge to this form of government in the US in recent times. When we see scenes of a "mob" breaking into the Capitol building with the aim of murdering someone who does not follow the "leader's" instructions, then it suggests insurrection by a few rather than election by all the people. When the "leader" describes them as "beautiful people" then there is a major challenge to the operation of a democracy which follows the system of power and legitimacy residing in the will of the whole population.

On the other hand, the systems which are based on the Westminster system (British) do not have that hiatus, that blockage. Here the law makers are the ones who make the law and also have the job of putting it into practice. Where there are two houses of parliament or Congress, there is usually some relatively easy way of finding a compromise or getting an agreement. It works well too in that significant improvements are often made as a result of discussions in each House. Nations where these systems exist are Britain (obviously), Canada, Australia, New Zealand and possibly India, Pakistan, Nigeria and Malaysia and any other nation which had extended colonial links with Britain. The important difference is that the Executive is not directly elected by the people and has only very limited reserve powers. In Britain there is an hereditary Executive (the Queen or King). In some other places, the executive is the same person and is represented by a Governor-General who is appointed by mutual agreement of the major leaders of the Legislature. Other Nations who follow the same principles of the Westminster system appoint their own President, or some other name for the position, in what they call a republic. The Executive has only the role of signing the laws on the advice of the Prime Minister and they become active.

What the Founding Fathers in the US certainly got right is the election of members of the Legislature is a leap-frogging system; only one third of representatives retire at any election. This system means that they can take a longer view and, therefore, can plan for the implementation of legislation beyond the "three-year term" of representatives in Australia and many other countries. Being encouraged to think beyond the limited three-year term is a great benefit in the current era. Democracies need to be able to do this as many non-democratic nations gain considerable advantage from extended periods in power by the particular dictator or elite. The benefits of this system could be gained in those nations where it is not the case fairly easily and it is one specific change I recommend as a significant benefit to all democracies.

I believe the Westminster system of government at core, has the necessary checks and balances to ensure the continuation of the form of government without the need for violent revolution to achieve desired changes. It allows for the form of government to be called a republic without the weakness which can come from the separation of lawmakers from those putting them into effect. It is interesting to observe the similarities between those values espoused by Christ and those which underpin a democracy. It is clearly the case that both have the same origin.

Another issue is that of the need for electors to actually vote. I am most familiar with the system where all electors MUST vote or face some punitive action like a fine. I have no strong opinion on this although I believe that it is better that all vote, even if they vote informally or mark the voting paper in a way that is unacceptable; like "I don't want to vote", or worse. That is still an expression of opinion which is of some value to the government of the day.

While it might be said that I congratulate myself as being in a better system than most, there is an issue which has gained a lot of currency in recent times. In what way can we recognise our first nation peoples in our constitution and give them a significant role in our government. At this stage, all I can present is the view that it is about time we did this. The how is not clear to me and it will take a lot of listening and debate until all of us can agree on the changes to our constitution which must be made for it to include something more than lip service to the idea. Those of us who have migrated to this wonderful place in the last two hundred plus years have made a system of government which suits us very well. It represents the normal invasion and conquest of the land and its peoples – to the victors the spoils. We need to do better and provide for a system where all of us get a fair share of what the land has provided through the efforts of all of us, not just the victors in an invasion. A lot of listening must be done and for most of us that has only just started. Let's get on with it and be creative so we can become the genuinely egalitarian nation we see ourselves to be.

Make it right the first time!

It puzzles me that others do not seem to understand that making the bed is a really simple task that needs to be done once a week. On other days it is just a matter of pulling up the top layer(s) of bedclothes and making them straight. That means they are ready for getting back in without much effort or for a tidy to meet some other requirement. Other methods of bed making seem, invariably, to require a total remake every day. I am a really lazy person when it comes to the daily chores. Thinking about it, in almost any situation. (I hear my friends and former colleagues yelling, "Not true! Not true!)

This underlying attitude, of making it easy, has been a major factor throughout my life and has been my downfall in many situations. School was always easy and I did things with the minimum of effort. As a result, much of the background reading required to gain a deeper understanding of the issues at stake was never done. As an example, I recall using the strategy in my History tutorials at University of adopting a totally outrageous position in response to the question and then spending the rest of the tutorial meeting defending it. The benefit was that I gained a really good grasp of the major relevant issues and could then write the paper with minimum effort. I passed and that was all I was really concerned about. The depth of my knowledge was slim indeed yet the result was that I managed to achieve a degree and two diplomas.

I shot myself in the foot though when preparing professional performances of opera or even just in choirs. It was only after falling short at critical times that I came to understand that it really was necessary to make the effort to get it just right and with confidence and nothing to provide assistance. As I recall, I made that effort only twice in my career as a singer. The result was a most satisfied feeling and general acclaim. My general slackness meant that the possibility of a professional career as a singer never materialised and the inane efforts I made to be creative in a number of other business efforts came to nothing. However, my directing of school musicals and three films that were presented to the public were a different kettle of fish. For some reason I became quite obsessive about them and prepared them in a fastidious manner and some might criticise them as over directed. The students and community participants who were the cast and crew seemed really to enjoy the solidity my preparation provided. It was the case for one production that the basics I had laid down provided for much improvisation by the cast. In most cases those innovations in rehearsal became part of the final show. We all thoroughly enjoyed ourselves.

But I digress from my major topic of bed making. It really is so simple. People who have been trained to make beds in such institutions as hospitals and nursing homes may have different ways of making a bed. I insist that this is a better way if the purpose is to leave it made for a week. When the bed will need to be changed more frequently, other considerations may apply.

To begin, spread the bottom sheet over the mattress so that it is aligned equally on each side <u>with one end of the sheet level with the bottom of the mattress.</u> This provides a lot to tuck in at the top and make a firm fitting so it does not work its way down during the life of the sheet change. I repeat, **level with the bottom of the mattress.** That's right, **level with the bottom.** It will stay there, I promise, if you do what I say.

Then, tuck the top of the sheet around the top of the mattress so there is the same width on either side. The method of tucking in the top corners is critical. What I term "hospital corners" make a very firm and reliable hold. The hospital corner is made by taking the side of the sheet in one hand, level with the top end of the mattress and stretching it out at the same horizontal as the top of the mattress. This will make a diagonal of the lower level of the sheet from that hand to the corner of the mattress. Half way along this diagonal, using the other hand, fold the sheet under so a right angle is made between the top surface of the mattress and the sheet hanging down. Allow the sheet then to fall over your hand and then tuck it in firmly along the length of the side.

Reading that back left me totally confused and lost. That is the opposite of what I want to achieve. Hence, I will provide some photos to assist.

Spread the bottom sheet with one end at the foot of the mattress as shown.

That's right! One end of the sheet level with the bottom of the mattress! I really mean that. The sheet will be held in place by what you do at the top! Got it? One end of the sheet level with the bottom of the mattress. Nothing, **nothing** over the end! And **evenly hanging down each side**.

Tuck the top of the sheet in at the head of the mattress; right round the head of the mattress and then make the corner as shown; the first stage of a "hospital corner.

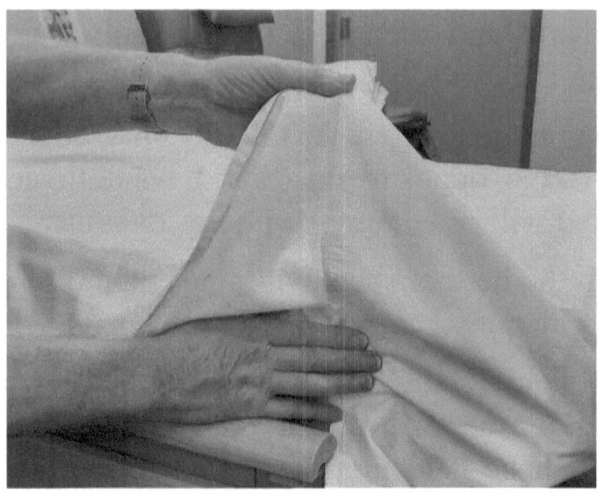

Then fold down as shown.

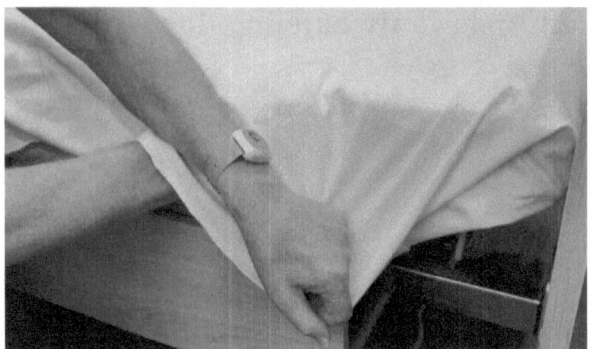

Complete the corner and then do the same on the other side.

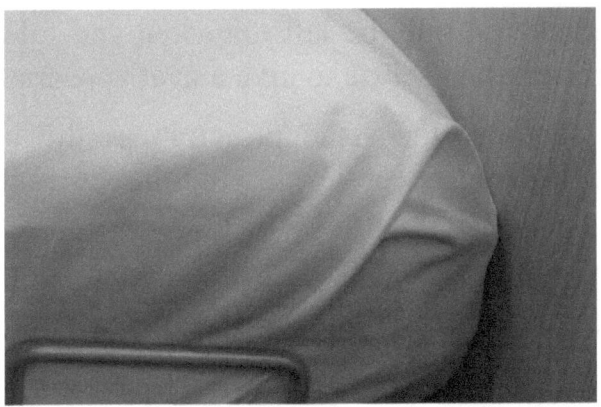

The sides are tucked in for the full length of the mattress so the sheet is firmly and smoothly located on the mattress. (It is not really a necessity to follow the military test of bouncing a coin on the sheet to see if it is firmly held in place.) This method ensures the sheet will stay in place until it is time to change it again.

The top sheet is then spread smoothly over the mattress so that the **top** of the sheet is level with the **top** of the mattress and each side of the sheet hangs equally down the sides. The sides of the top sheet and blanket(s) may be left untucked and folded up underneath themselves to give a neat appearance.

It's essentially the same principle as the bottom sheet. **Bottom** sheet level with the **bottom**; **top** sheet level with the **top** of the mattress.

Use the same "hospital corner" technique to tuck in the bottom corners of the top sheet.

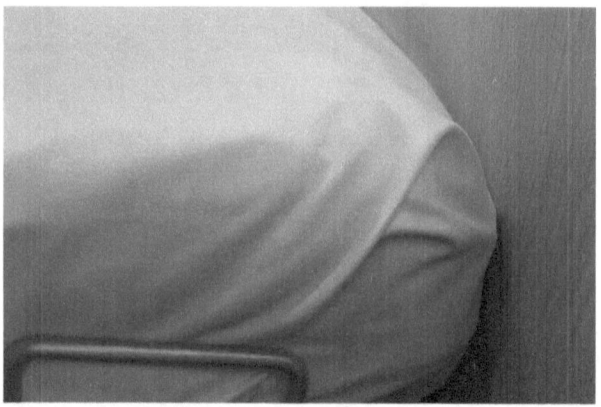

Then finish the top sheet as shown.

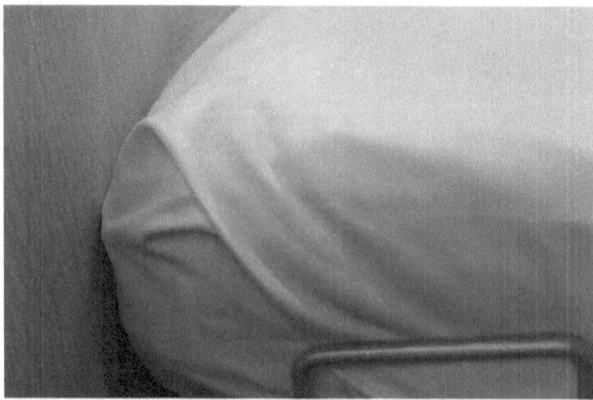

The use of blankets requires a similar technique as

described for the top sheet. The only difference might be that the end of the blanket might be about halfway up the pillow distance. (Keeping your shoulders warm is a good idea.) The top sheet and blankets may be tucked together although it may prove more convenient to tuck them separately.

This method of bed making was developed with the assistance of "camps" at the local RAAF base when I was a student, my experiences as a student in the school boarding house and considerable years with my wife.

What I really wanted to discuss is the principle of getting it right the first time; the careful approach that saves time and effort in the long run even if it takes a little longer than it might at the immediate moment. That is the very idea that did not occur to me until I was venturing into creative tasks for which I had no training, just a keen desire to see it done.

Filmmaking was a new, demanding experience for me. I had a limited understanding of the process. In each case I was involved in the writing process at some stage. I understood that a storyboard and detailed analysis of all aspects of the process needed to be completed. As a result, a detailed document was produced which provided information about the appearance of the shot or the location, any props needed, the characters (if any), or any other necessary information to make the filming and preparations for it an easier task. That document became the reference to guide the process of making the film. Scheduling of the various sections became much easier and all filming became a set of simple tasks, easily managed.

The editing process was a set of small tasks made easier by the detailed preparation at the beginning.

Marketing and promotion were never a necessity as two of the films were in the video format and intended for broadcast by the local TV station. Any promotion was therefore part of their responsibility and it was dealt with as part of normal broadcast content.

The earlier film was made for the Theatre Organ Society and had a defined audience; the local fans of theatre organ music and its accompaniment to films. The parents and friends of the cast were also part of the audience so they could see their children on screen.

The whole point of this chapter is the realisation that "getting it right the first time" is the best way to achieve anything of substantive value. What has become a platitude now, "That life is not a dress rehearsal, it's the opening night; all the time", really is true. It's so easy to stuff it up and sometimes so difficult to repair. All of us make mistakes, and usually they can be corrected without too much difficulty. There are some though, that are almost impossible. Some decisions need to be given considerable and careful thought. Drastic action must only be taken when careful analysis of the issues is made. I know I stuffed it up, and beating myself up is another issue.

Eckart Tolle[36] has made a significant contribution to understanding that there is only the present in which action can be taken; there is little point in wanting to change what you have done or how you might do it in the future. We have all been guilty of beating ourselves up over the things we really stuffed up. THERE'S NO POINT! Get over it and move on, even if it is really difficult and you really want to "fix it" and get it right. It's so easy to be wise in hindsight. The only value of looking at events of the past is that they will provide us with some guidance as what to do in the now. (Hence the study of History is an essential part of every one's education; for example, we want no repeat of Neville Chamberlain's "Appeasement" policy, in very similar situations. Political leaders MUST be guided by the lessons of History, not by simple considerations of Law or ideology. But that is another topic for consideration elsewhere.)

One might conclude that I reckon something new is too hard to contemplate. Far from it. Being bold is

---

[36] Eckhart Tolle, *The Power of Now,* 1997, Namaste Publishing, Vancouver

exciting and rewarding of itself. On most occasions, boldness will be rewarded with success, provided there is thorough preparation and alertness to different needs is exercised along the way. Sounds like I am hedging my bets? You would too if you had received a diagnosis of Multiple Sclerosis; tends to make one draw back a bit. It also can really screw up one's thinking, so that must be taken into account. Careful consideration of the advice of trusted friends is really important before taking any action.

But I get distracted again. I consider it really important to get the exhortation, "Get it right the first time. Make the extra effort. It will save time, money and work by doing so." This principle can be a slogan to use throughout one's life. I look back and see there are so many things I would do differently if I could have the opportunity to go back and have another go. Beating oneself up about it is what is most likely if I did.

Which brings me to a very important aid in getting over this problem; remove two words from my thinking and use; *should* and *ought*. If either is used it implies judgement. In either case, there is the idea that something is wrong with what has happened. There is nothing that can be done to change it now. One might consider that it could be done better if a similar situation occurred in the future. Nothing can be done now! And I have already used a replacement word; *could*. *Could* and *might* can be used to good effect in changing thinking to a much more useful and beneficial outcome. For example; "I could have written that into the agreement" rather than "I should have . . . . . ."

Of course, the use of a fitted bottom sheet and a quilt or doona or duvet, or whatever you know it as, makes all this palaver[37] irrelevant. Nonetheless, getting it right the first time is a very good maxim to guide your attitude. But don't let it stop you from trying things out to see if they work!

The teachings of Christ help us "Get it right the first time" through their recommendations regarding prayer and decision-making. Following them gives us the necessary contemplative period and a much higher likelihood of success. If only . . . . . . But that is beating myself up on the mistakes I made in the past and which I can do nothing to change. Those decisions were made in the circumstances which existed then, not now, with the benefit of 20/20 hindsight vision.

Much to my chagrin!

I also note in hindsight that it is not surprising I could not manage my classes successfully because I adopted a **Victim Mentality**. Students are intuitive and they are quick to take advantage. This is why

---

[37] A word which can loosely be translated as "useless carry on".

so many students are bullied; They feel that "poor me" will get them through life. Lest the reader comes to think I believe that the bullied bring it on themselves, I don't. Bullying is unacceptable in any circumstance. It will have the opposite effect on the attitudes of the bullied in that they are likely to be worse in their belief that "poor me" is the only way. All efforts need to be made to achieve a far more positive attitude to life; "poor me" is a very unhelpful attitude to take and leads only to unsatisfactory outcomes.

You want what?

To be HAPPY!!!!!????

It seems the pursuit of happiness occupies a lot of our time, energy and mental capacity. So much so there have been many books written about the "How to achieve it" and why you may be feeling something other than happy. It is even enshrined in the Declaration of Independence of the USA: "We hold these truths to be self-evident, that <u>all men are created equal</u>, that they are endowed by their Creator with certain unalienable Rights, that among these are <u>Life, Liberty and the pursuit of Happiness</u>."

In Matthew 5:3 Jesus is quoted as stating that; "Blessed are the poor in spirit, for theirs is the kingdom of heaven.[38]"

The Amplified version expands the meaning of the word "Blessed" as being happy, to be envied & spiritually prosperous with life - joy & satisfaction in God's favour & salvation, regardless of their outward conditions.

According to *Psychology Today*, University of California Professor Sonja Lyubomirsky[39] states,

---

[38] New International Version (NIV)
[39] Professor Lyubomirsky, Ph.D., is Professor of Psychology at the University of California, Riverside. She has completed much research and many books and articles about the "scientific pursuit of happiness". She has given her consent to

"40 per cent of our capacity for happiness is within our power to change."

If this is true, and it is, there's hope for us all. There are billions of people on our planet and clearly some are truly happy. The rest of us bounce back and forth between happiness and unhappiness depending on the day.

I use the seven qualities that she identifies of chronically unhappy people, with her discussion of them, as the basis for examining what the Bible says about what we can do. Her work is well supported by my limited findings and is probably more acceptable to many people in our society because she is a contemporary author rather than someone who wrote thousands of years ago. I make no claim to being an authority on what the Bible teaches, just that I know some of what it contains which is so useful in guiding our way to live. Ms Lyubomirsky has written much literature on the subject of happiness, based on her extensive research. I commend her web site to anyone seeking a modern, in-depth analysis of the topic of happiness and how to be it. Also, the website which I have found most useful is https://www.openbible.info/topics/. There are others that may prove of greater use to the reader.

---

the inclusion of her material here.

The Seven Qualities of Unhappy People

1. Your default belief is that life is hard.

Happy people know life can be hard and tend to bounce through hard times with an attitude of curiosity versus victimhood. They take responsibility for how they got themselves into a mess, and focus on getting themselves out of it as soon as possible.

Perseverance towards problem-solving versus complaining over circumstances is a symptom of a happy person. Unhappy people see themselves as victims of life and stay stuck in the "look what happened to me" attitude versus finding a way through and out the other side.

"as a man thinks in his heart so is he.[40]"

It is always possible to decide to find the good in a situation, regardless of how dire it might seem. Changing our thinking can be hard work but never 'too hard' and the result is always worth it. We can also refer to Paul's experience in prison. He and Silas had been imprisoned and were singing psalms and praising God when there was an earthquake and all the doors flew open. What an excellent example of it being worth choosing to be grateful and happy. They were even praising God and

---

[40] PRV23:7 (PART A)

singing hymns![41] The really noteworthy result of their prayers and singing was that the prison doors came open and they were set free. An extra benefit was to the jailer and his family in that they too were set free from being stuck in their guilt for all the things they had done which fell short of their own beliefs about what they might have been. Clearly, life might be hard, yet that is no reason not to choose to be happy. The result is a better life.

2. You believe most people can't be trusted.

I won't argue that healthy discernment is unimportant, but most happy people are trusting of their fellow man. They believe in the good in people, versus assuming everyone is out to get them. Generally open and friendly towards people they meet, happy people foster a sense of community around themselves and meet new people with an open heart.

Unhappy people are distrustful of most people they meet and assume that strangers can't be trusted. Unfortunately, this behaviour slowly starts to close the door on any connection outside of an inner-circle and thwarts all chances of meeting new friends.

---

[41] Acts 16:25-29

A part of the key commandment that Christ gave was to "love your neighbour as yourself". Christian life is about letting people in. In to the point they become family and when we get there, (through the let downs and disappointments sometimes people give us) we come out the other side with those people as family and on our side when we need them most. This is how we "love our neighbours as ourselves". Hence, if we want to be happy, our best benefit is to trust others as they earn that trust rather than maintaining suspicion of their honesty. The result is to become ever more secure in this world with many friends and family who are trusted and who trust us.

This does not mean that a new acquaintance is given the keys to the house and car and safety deposit box. A healthy discernment can be expected and it is clearly wrong to put temptation in the way of the unknown. The "taking of responsibility" phrase recurs in this book and it is appropriate here as well; to take responsibility for ensuring that sensible appraisal should be given to new acquaintances for the best benefit of all.

    YOU WERE NOT MEANT TO FIGHT ALONE.

3. You concentrate on what's wrong in this world versus what's right.

There's plenty wrong with this world, no arguments

here, yet unhappy people turn a blind eye to what's actually right in this world and instead focus on what's wrong. You can spot them a mile away; they'll be the ones complaining and responding to any positive attributes of our world with "yeah but".

Happy people are aware of global issues, but balance their concern with also seeing what's right. I like to call this keeping both eyes open. Unhappy people tend to close one eye towards anything good in this world in fear they might be distracted from what's wrong. Happy people keep it in perspective. They know our world has problems and they also keep an eye on what's right.

You can also tell the people who are looking at what's wrong by the lines they have on their faces. They are usually much deeper.

It seems to me that those who are concerned most with what is wrong are those who are easily led into fear of what might be or look only at a few examples which support their view of things. It is most unfortunate that there are quite unprincipled people who massage the events so they seem to be indicative of a world that is a dangerous place, rather than a place where opportunities abound for all sorts of really wonderful things to happen. Fear is a really easy emotion to invoke for such unprincipled people. It is really sad to see another so fearful of what might happen that they become incapable of any enjoyment or any real achievement. Christ taught a much different view. He asked the question "And which of you by being anxious can add a single hour to his span of life?[42]" as part of a longer discussion of the loss of productivity occurring as a result of anxiety and worry.

A few other references which suggest we could live free of worry are "Casting all your anxieties on him, because he cares for you.[43]" and "Trust in the Lord with all your heart, and do not lean on your own understanding.[44]"There are many more.

4. You compare yourself to others and harbour jealousy.

Unhappy people believe someone else's good fortune steals from their own. They believe there's not enough goodness to go around and constantly compare yours against theirs. This leads to jealousy and resentment.

Happy people know that your good luck and circumstance are merely signs of what they too can aspire to achieve. Happy people believe they carry

---

[42] Matthew 6:27
[43] 1 Peter 5:7
[44] Proverbs 3:5

a unique blueprint that can't be duplicated or stolen from — by anyone on the planet. They believe in unlimited possibilities and don't get bogged down by thinking one person's good fortune limits their possible outcome in life.

There are numerous references in the Bible that strongly advise against comparing oneself with others, both favourably and with envy or self-deprecation. Solomon, whom many consider to be the wisest man who ever lived, wrote the Proverbs and this issue appears many times there. "A sound heart is life to the body, but envy is rottenness to the bones.[45]" The topic appears several times in Chapters 26 and 27. Examples are; "Do you see a man who is wise in his own eyes? There is more hope for a fool than for him.[46]" and "The sluggard is wiser in his own eyes than seven men who can answer sensibly.[47]"

Solomon wrote many generations before Christ. In the Gospels Christ taught against it often. Perhaps the best example is in Matthew 20: 24-28 that is; "And when the ten heard it, they were indignant at the two brothers. But Jesus called them to him and said; 'You know that the rulers of the Gentiles lord it over them,

---

[45] Proverbs 14:30
[46] Proverbs 26:12
[47] Proverbs 26:16

and their great ones exercise authority over them. It shall not be so among you. But whoever would be great among you must be your servant, and whoever would be first among you must be your slave, even as the Son of Man came not to be served but to serve, and to give his life as a ransom for many.'" Another example of Christ's attitude to the idea of comparing oneself to others may be found in Luke 18:9-14 where He said the person who humbled himself was much closer to God than the righteous person who had spent his life studying the scriptures and Law.

It was Paul, perhaps the man most responsible for the establishment and early growth of the Christian church, who wrote of this as well in many of the letters to churches all over the Middle East. Those letters contain much advice about how to live our lives happily. Some interpret what he wrote as very restrictive and puritanical. I suggest that he can be read in a very different way in our world rather than in the world of first century Palestine in which he lived and wrote. There are a number of scholars who have translated the Bible in language that is much more in tune with the modern world. The letters of Paul become far more acceptable as guides for us when we read what they have translated the original language to mean. The intent of Paul has not been lost. Rather it has been communicated in language that makes much more sense to us[48].

The Bible also contains much advice about you and how valuable and unique you are; that God has made you especially for the purposes God has in mind. **It is your job to find out what they are and get on with it.** You are the only person who can be you and you are special because of it. There is no need to make any comparison with others because they cannot be you. Only you can do that.

5. *You strive to control your life.*

There's a difference between control and striving to achieve our goals. Happy people take steps daily to achieve their goals, but realise in the end, there's very little control over what life throws their way.

Unhappy people tend to micromanage in effort to control all outcomes and fall apart in dramatic display when life throws a wrench in their plan. Happy people can be just as focused, yet still have the ability to go with the flow and not melt down when life delivers a curve-ball.

The key here is to be goal-oriented and focused, but allow room for letting sh*t happen without falling

---

[48] Eugene H. Peterson *The Message* is one example. There are others which use a less vernacular language and seem to be more "biblical" in tone.

apart when the best laid plans go awry- because they will. Going with the flow is what happy people have as plan B.

If we strive to control our lives so that all we set our hearts on eventuates, we are guaranteed to fail. Life has its own way of bringing us into that place of failure where we are unable to achieve what we set our hearts on. We have a much healthier approach taught by the Bible in many references. "Do not be anxious about tomorrow, for tomorrow will be anxious for itself. Sufficient for the day is its own trouble[49]". And, "For whoever would save his life will lose it, but whoever loses his life for my sake will find it[50]." Finally, Paul writes some really good advice in Philippians: "Don't fret or worry. Instead of worrying, pray. Let petitions and praises shape your worries into prayers, letting God know your concerns. Before you know it, a sense of God's wholeness, everything coming together for good, will come and settle you down. It's wonderful what happens when Christ displaces worry at the center of your life.[51]"

Fairly clearly, we do ourselves no favours if we set out to be totally in control of our lives so we cannot cope when what we want does not appear. It is much healthier to be able to accept all that comes

---

[49] Matthew 6:34
[50] Matthew 16:25
[51] Phil 4:6-7

regardless of whether it is part of our plan or not. We are much better able to deal with all that life might throw at us and act to make the best of whatever occurs. Of course, expressing gratitude is always healthy and beneficial.

6. *You consider your future with worry and fear.*

There's only so much rent space between your ears. Unhappy people fill their thoughts with what could go wrong versus what might go right.

Happy people take on a healthy dose of delusion and allow themselves to daydream about what they'd like to have life unfold for them. Unhappy people fill that head space with constant worry and fear.

Happy people experience fear and worry, but make an important distinction between feeling it and living it. When fear or worry crosses a happy person's mind, they'll ask themselves if there's an action they can take to prevent their fear or worry from happening (there's responsibility again) *and they take it. If not, they realise they're spinning in fear and they lay it down.*

It seems to me that the word FEAR is one of the worst in the language. It is often given much greater credibility than it deserves, particularly when it is applied to what might happen. One of the now overused acronyms can make the reality appear much more likely and help reduce the emotion attached to the word. That acronym is: **F**alse **E**vidence **A**ppearing **R**eal. I suggest that the fear and worry will make the undesired more likely to happen. Consider the cyclist. A rock appears in the road. Fearing it will cause an accidental fall, he looks at it closely, just to ensure he does not hit it. Since we tend to steer where we are looking, he hits the rock and falls off instead of looking at the road adjacent and missing it completely.

The origins of fear for a person are in the memories of unpleasant, or worse, experiences. In some cases, professional help is needed to enable those experiences to be seen in a manner that allows life to progress with positive expectation. For most people it is possible to overcome bad memories by:

(1) reframing them. One manner of dealing with the experience is to look at what benefits have occurred as a result. I look back at the experience of going over the edge of the Gillies Highway[52] near Cairns in that it meant I had to replace my car with one that had automatic transmission. My ability to operate the clutch had declined so it was nearly a necessity. The Bible has an example here with the

---

[52] See chapter on Encounters

story of Joseph who had been sold by his brothers into slavery. Looking back, Joseph said, 'You meant evil against me, but God meant it for good.'[53]

(2) Reject them. The next time a bad memory resurfaces, refuse to entertain it. That might sound impossible. Indeed, it may be difficult. The simple solution is to give your mind something else to think about; perhaps the really good things also associated with them. Isaiah suggests we 'Do not...ponder the things of the past[54].'

(3) Refocus your thoughts. This was suggested in the previous point and it means more than that. Finding something good to look forward to will always give your spirits a lift. Something as mundane as the taste of dinner that you will cook tonight can be enough to get you back on the track of being a happy person again. Paul had much to write about this, including: 'Forgetting those things which are behind and reaching forward to those things which are ahead.[55]' You say, 'I can't help remembering.' If you can recall your troubles, you can recall your blessings.

The story is that being fearful of the future makes for a distressing present and makes the future more

---

[53] Genesis 50:20 NAS
[54] Isaiah 43:18 NAS
[55] Philippians 3:13 NKJV

likely to fulfil what you had been worried about. Taking a more positive approach to the future will almost certainly mean a happier life now as well as in the future.

Rather than considering your future with worry and fear, the Bible suggests: "If God gives such attention to the appearance of wildflowers—most of which are never even seen—don't you think he'll attend to you, take pride in you, do his best for you? What I'm trying to do here is to get you to relax, to not be so preoccupied with getting, so you can respond to God's giving. People who don't know God and the way he works fuss over these things, but you know both God and how he works. Steep your life in God-reality, God-initiative, God-provisions. Don't worry about missing out. You'll find all your everyday human concerns will be met."[56]

7. You fill your conversations with gossip and complaints. (This is not only bad, but here we see it's actually bad for you!!!)

Unhappy people like to live in the past. What's happened to them and life's hardships are their conversation of choice. When they run out of things

---

[56] Matthew 6:30-33 The Message

to say, they'll turn to other people's lives and gossip.

Happy people live in the now and dream about the future. You can feel their positive vibe from across the room. They're excited about something they're working on, grateful for what they have and dreaming about the possibilities of life.

Obviously, none of us are perfect. We're all going to swim in negative waters once in a while, but what matters is how long we stay there and how quickly we work to get ourselves out. Practicing positive habits daily is what sets happy people apart from unhappy people, not doing everything perfectly.

Walk, fall down, get back up again, repeat. It's in the getting back up again where all the difference resides.

Control of what one says is really in your mind, your power. What you say says so much about who you are. Do you want to be known as a person who tells stories about others that are nothing to do with anyone else? What sort of friend would you be, that you tell others stories behind their back? What is more, how much fun is it to be regaled with the latest complaint about whatever might be not as it

SHOULD[57] be. I know my first thought is to flee from such a one.

James has something useful to say about this. "My friends, this can't go on. A spring doesn't gush fresh water one day and brackish the next, does it? Apple trees don't bear strawberries, do they? Raspberry bushes don't bear apples, do they? You're not going to dip into a polluted mud hole and get a cup of clear, cool water, are you?[58]" It seems that what we say needs to be closely guarded if we are to prosper.

James again: "This is scary: You can tame a tiger, but you can't tame a tongue—it's never been done. The tongue runs wild, a wanton killer. With our tongues we bless God our Father; with the same tongues we curse the very men and women God made in God's image. Curses and blessings out of the same mouth![59]" Clearly, there is an issue we must address for our best benefit. Controlling our tongue so it does not express wanton complaints and gossips about others is of best benefit to oneself and also the subjects of your gossip.

Think about it. Unhappiness is not due to events. It

---

[57] It would be better if the words 'should' and 'ought' were to be not part of our thinking at all. They always imply that a judgment has been made. We have no right to make judgment of another.

[58] James 3: 10-12 The Message

[59] James 3: 7-10 The Message

is due to symptoms and vice versa. Happiness is also not due to events but due to symptoms. You therefore have the choice of symptoms; you are in control of what you feel!

You can use the above to self-diagnose where you are at, what symptoms do you have? If symptoms of unhappiness then start to apply the medicine found in this book or, even, perhaps, God's word. Let your perspectives on life be changed and you will find your tone (happiness or unhappiness) will get changed in the process.

Most importantly, the feelings of happiness are a choice on our part. We choose what to do or not do, we choose what to think or not think, we choose what to believe or not believe. Each of these choices is ours to make and no one else's. Each of them has an impact on our happiness. Each of them is fundamental to who we are. Different things make different people happy so we are really best situated when we let God lead us in our choices. Like any Father, God wants only the best for us. That BEST is for us to choose in the light of all that has been made available to us. Best of all, the feeling of happiness is a choice as well. Even in the most dire of situations, we can choose to be happy. Having made that choice, we can speak it into truth through the use of what have come to be called affirmations. We can choose to speak and behave as if we are happy and it will be so.

This chapter has also demonstrated that the Bible contains real solutions to real, current problems. For those people who are sceptical that they cannot find the answers within the Bible, the technology we have now makes it easy to search the Bible to get texts that are relevant to whatever is of concern. Begin by entering "search bible topics" into your search engine and then use one of the options that appear. Each will have the means of searching the whole Bible for the topic you enter. It then becomes a selection of text that seems to fit the problem best. I explore the Bible as a pathway to life in a number of situations in much of this book.

Do you want more?

Men! You are missing out.

Most of us never realise what is available to us from the woman who is a part of our life because we do not recognise a critical part of what we have to give. It is most often the case that the woman does not know what she has to give either because the man she has chosen/accepted has never provided the stimulus and she does not know what is possible; she has never experienced it. I consider this chapter to be, perhaps, the most important of the book.

So, men, it's up to you.

To all men! How big and strong do you feel when you can bully the woman you married and therefore one might expect to love? Do you really get off on doing that? Are you not in a partnership? Why not be conscious that you do have a woman to love and cherish, that bullying her in any way is counter-productive for the relationship and to the way she is likely to respond to you? I suppose you would also expect her to provide you with great sex whenever you feel like it whether she wants or not; when she has just been bullied into submission on something else. Perhaps you are not aware that you can get absolutely fantastic sex if you treat her with love, with respect, to the foreplay you see as being rather unnecessary because you can "go for it" at the drop of a bra strap, or similar, so why can't she? If this is you, it is highly likely you will have stopped reading before you got to this point because you are so self-absorbed that your wife's feelings and thoughts are irrelevant to you if they are barriers to you getting what you want.

It is so easy to become so absorbed in your own thoughts that you can cross over anything your spouse may be thinking without even being aware of it. This could be the cause of mirth where you trust each other and can speak without rancour in such a situation. On the other hand, it could lead to a major flare up of conflicting emotions. The way to avoid the latter is to recognise what has happened and apologise immediately without reservation. It helps if there has been a history of genuine respect and unconditional love that has been clearly shown. It can easily become the basis for mirth and a loving make-up.

The topic of marriage has been canvassed widely in a variety of media and I enter this area with trepidation. There are many authors and commentators who have addressed this with a great deal of wisdom and sensitivity. What the more recent authors and commentators have been emphasising have been the values of the partners in the relationship and the way that affects what happens.

It is my intention to explore the potential of that relationship and some ways people might set out on a path of increasing intimacy through the "seasons" of life. My exploration is based on my own experience, the views of some of the commentators I have read or heard, discussions with a number of people and the development of a personal set of beliefs about my best way of making a successful relationship. Along the way I will signpost what I have found to be valuable tools in my own development as a human, a man and more lately, as a committed Christian. I think it most useful to remember what Paul wrote in Galatians 5:22: "But the **fruit of the Spirit** is love, joy, peace, long suffering, gentleness, goodness, faith."[60] That is something I could easily use to beat myself up.

The Bible is one area where the topic has been addressed because of its centrality to the procreation of the species, if nothing else. **It is, of course, possible to read what the Bible has to say without becoming a Christian. It is a very useful manual for life.**

The way it is addressed in the Old Testament was appropriate in the society that existed then, when polygamy was the norm rather than the exception and illegal. When we take what Paul says about the relationship in his letters, we find a careful

---

[60] Galatians 5:22 has been translated in many different ways in English. Nonetheless, the ones chosen are similar in intent and meaning.

exposition of the specific roles played by each of the genders. Modern commentators have found his views very sexist and undervaluing of the role of the female of the species. That view is popular yet there is much of what Paul describes about the relationship that emphasises the beauty of what it can mean, without setting out to do so. It is not my intention here to produce an academic treatise on the views of Paul. I am in no way qualified to do that since I cannot read what Paul wrote in the language in which he wrote it. That would be a minimum for such analysis.

At the outset I have to state that I have been divorced. However, I am a good friend with my former wife. I have remarried and that is an endorsement of much that I write here. I reckon I now would be a far better husband than I ever was when I was first married. Not only was it a major concern for me that the deterioration of my mobility and other bodily functions due to multiple sclerosis led to a very dim assessment of my value as a marriage partner and therefore led to my divorce, but also a very low self-assessment of my attractiveness to form a new relationship. In one sense, at least, I did not want to inflict myself on a woman at this stage of her life, assuming she would be of a similar age to myself, in her mid-sixties. Who am I to say anything about that, really?

Having got that out of the way, I believe that it is possible for a relationship between a man and a woman to be more intimate, joy filled and beneficial than any other connection that might be possible. I look back on the thirty-three years of my first marriage and realise I just did not understand what was possible until I had taken myself out of it. That is not looking back with rose coloured glasses at all, although I certainly miss many bits of what we had. I think I would never have come to understand how good a relationship could be if I had stayed in that marriage. I needed the space and separation to "grow up", as the Pastor at my church, said. It is one of the lessons of life that, as part of "getting somewhere" is the realisation that the journey has always only just begun, to a different place; in this case, deeper understanding[61].

A good starting point for this discussion is a careful analysis of oneself and the expectations one brings to a potential relationship. Every one of us would do well to start with a really large meal of "humble pie". The arrogance of the attitude that "I am right and therefore you must be wrong" is a certain foundation for resentment that may take a long time to build to exploding point. That is nonetheless a

---

[61] The same applies in the relationship I have with God and His Son Jesus; it keeps on deepening as I open new "doors" or "pathways".

certain outcome. One of those useful tools I have used is the Enneagram. It is the oldest of the "personality typing" systems which have been created, being about 5000 years old. It has been analysed and developed in the modern era and provides a very useful understanding of what some of the processing of information and motivations for action are for each of us. It is at this point I will make a statement that will probably be repeated in various contexts. There can be no judgement on the basis of the enneagram. It is just information to inform action, not judgement. The case against judgementalism is very strong and judging others is best left somewhere else, outside the relationship.

I am moved by the contacts I have had with women who have been badly hurt by events that have been part of their lives, in some cases at the earliest stages of life. In some cases, it is also part of an adulthood that has been far less than joyful. In almost all cases they have erected emotional "walls" in an effort to protect themselves from similar hurts in the future. As is well established, these walls are much more than protection. They are also barriers to the love, joy and connection with others that we all really seek. It seems to me that the only way of letting go or setting oneself free from these barriers and the hurts which are their foundation, is to forgive, in some cases, the unforgivable. An alternative in those cases might be to erect a wall around the hurt and isolate it from current experiences so it becomes possible to be free and joy filled again.

Another of the very valuable tools I have used is The Journey, created by Brandon Bays[62]. This set of tools encourages people to delve into their experiences and get in touch with old traumatic memories that are stored at a cellular level and have the opportunity to clear these completely. There is a website and books written by Brandon Bays which give so much better detail about this set of tools. There are accredited practitioners who can provide skilled guidance on your "Journeys" which are designed to ensure that one's growth to real freedom progresses apace. A similar result can be achieved through developing a deep and very personal relationship with Jesus. I found it most useful to begin with the Journey because it led me to that deeper relationship I have with Christ now. Some will find that continuing with The Journey suits them better. They are not mutually exclusive.

---

[62] The first of Brandon's books is *The Journey* which lays out what became the foundation for a set of very valuable tools which can be very useful in setting people free of the blocks and limitations we all have. This has been followed by a number of others. I commend them all as well as the use of the set of tools with a qualified practitioner, found on the website *www.thejourney.com* or with the addition of the letters denoting the desired country.

As a man I am often stirred to outrage by the behaviour of men towards the women who are closest to them; their wives, mothers and daughters. It is the case that people who make the decision to become half of a marriage will make their own best attempt at succeeding in creating a lasting and mutually beneficial relationship. There are, however, some basic principles that need to be followed if that relationship is to survive and prosper. Central to the relationship between two people is the honouring of the other and the desire to ensure the benefit for the other of one's behaviour. If both parties have this approach, it is a sure recipe for an ever-deepening love and joy in their lives. Let there be more of this in our community rather than the images we so often see of men being abusive, disrespectful in the extreme and irresponsible in their behaviour. The picture presented in the media is that men are laughably immature as well. Is it any wonder that women are so dissatisfied with their lot in life if they are not given the opportunities to be the shining lights they were born to be, even if it is within their own family and not in the public domain? The key role for the male of the relationship is to affirm his wife in all of the ways he can create. My strong suggestion for all men if they want to make their marriages so much better is to read and apply the thoughts

and recommendations of David Deida in his book, "The way of the Superior Man"[63] and to take to heart the words of Paul in Philippians to love and honour their wives.

Lest men feel that I am totally out of touch with the reality that exists in the behaviour of some women, I suggest that much of that is derived from the treatment they have received from the men in their lives. Viewing women through rose coloured glasses is not what I am recommending at all. I strongly suggest to men that they explore the value systems of potential mates very carefully and deeply to ensure that they can be matched to their own. The platitude, "decide in haste, regret at leisure" applies here for both genders. It is also the case that personality change cannot be made after the event. This is very likely true, even if a person believes it to be otherwise. Clear change must be demonstrated at a very deep level to be effective. Reverting to ingrained behaviour is most likely at some future time, leading to major stress in the relationship. For women, David Deida has written a different book, "Dear Lover"[64]. I strongly recommend both partners read both. That way there will be an understanding of what each is

---

[63] Deida, David *The way of the Superior Man* Paperback available on line and in some bookshops

[64] Deida, David *Dear Lover* Paperback available on line and in some bookshops

attempting. The danger here is that the information will be used to beat the other "over the head" and the "blame game" is begun. Commitments need to be made to NOT do that. One would hope that potential partners would enter discussions about the nature of a possible relationship well before entering one. In a perfect world, that might be the case always. It is not yet too late, probably.

One component of any relationship will be those occasions when conflict does arise. There are numerous responses available when it does; and it will. I can only recommend that each couple discuss how they will approach the resolution of it early rather than after it arises. One very helpful approach is to see it as an opportunity to find a deeper level in the relationship rather than allowing it to become the foundation of an edifice of resentment. One might rejoice at the appearance of conflict because of the opportunity it provides. The resolution to the satisfaction of both parties is the only real path if resentment is not to grow. Another helpful decision I have made is to learn to love those things that annoy me in the other partner. It works!!!

Honesty and openness are critical elements of a relationship. They follow the honouring of each other. As soon as there is any dishonesty in the relationship it seems that the seeds will grow and lead to uncertainty and distrust. Should it occur that one person is dishonest the only successful solution is to own up and clear it out so it does not fester and grow a plant of division in the relationship. Both parties need to be ready to forgive when the situation demands it if it is possible. It is an essential course of action and the sooner the better for the relationship. In a relationship where there is a genuine desire to honour and love the other, the likelihood of dishonesty entering is reduced although not excluded. The confession and desire for forgiveness must be sincere or the seeds continue to mature and grow until a situation of major fracture becomes likely. When it comes down to it, a careful review of the marriage vows is sometimes a very healthy course of action. That way it is highly likely that new understanding will occur as to what the couple are really doing together in the first place and is often helpful when there is a challenge to be overcome. I throw in here that my father thought it most important that there be a photograph of the wedding so that it would remind both partners of the vows or the decisions made. The re-iteration of the vows is similar to the reminiscences of the photograph.

Women need to remember that they are nearly all very nervous at some stage of their lives and particularly when they first have children. It is imperative that they support each other rather than make negative comments about the young and nervous mother. The father has a very important part to play here as well, encouraging and affirming his wife to ensure she feels his love is even deeper, if that is possible. It is very important that he is as present as is possible for the time during and after the birth, encouraging and affirming his wife. All of this must be genuine, else it will have a negative effect; the very opposite of what is intended.

For men, anointing the woman in your life with the words and behaviour you choose; affirming her through the ways that you express your feelings for her; making her feel so special that the only response possible is love, can only lead to a better and more fulfilling relationship for both partners in the relationship. My strong advice to men is to love your wife, even if you don't particularly feel like it right now. You will soon if you do and she will be a more than willing partner because you have made her feel so special that she wants more of that. The foundation, then, of the relationship is what is described as unconditional love. With the conscious decision to make this a part of the way you relate, it becomes very easy to make it the truth, even if there is some doubt at times.

It hardly needs to be said that there are desires and motivations that have no place within a marriage if it is to succeed. Greed, selfishness, self-centredness, dishonesty and lust[65] are but a few of these. If they are given free rein, the result is a rapid dissolution of the loving relationship that once existed. Bitterness and hurt are the sure result if either of the partners allows those to become a part of their attitudes within the relationship. The desired result that makes a marriage so worthwhile is lost and regret and pain take over.

Where the relationship is based on unconditional love and the desire to see it deepen and grow ever more intimate, it might well be the case that the way forward is a shared commitment to Christ. If both people have a personal relationship to Him, it is relatively easy then to surrender to each other as one has already to Him. That which is shared in Christ then magnifies the deepening intimacy between the partners. Physical and sexual intimacy then grow as well, making for a stronger and more joy filled relationship. Bring it on!!!! This is what is intended from marriage as an institution and it is available to all of us if we are prepared to decide that love is central to it. Of course, any children

---

[65] The physical desire for the other is normal and may be likened to lust. There is nothing wrong with expressing and experiencing those really powerful desires within the relationship in all their fullness. It needs to be within the framework of unconditional love so that it is not one partner *using* the other to satisfy their physical desires as opposed to sharing in the expression of that powerful desire.

then get the message as well and much of the hurt that exists in the world now would not occur.

It is also worth considering the possibility that one can learn to love those things that are found to be annoying. This was raised briefly earlier. Methodology is offered here. From personal experience, it is possible to make the decision to find the annoying to be sources of humour and love rather than to challenge the relationship. One thing is for certain; the possibility of changing those annoying things is quite remote and they could become a source of conflict. A better result is that they become a source of humour and love.

A different alternative might be to focus on those things that you love about the other so that the annoying fade into insignificance; they are over-ridden by the most appealing behaviours and qualities.

Bob and Debbie Gass may provide some assistance. They wrote "the Word for Today".

"The ten reasons people say they are unhappy

(1) They didn't think alike in many areas.

(2) They had little insight into each other's feelings.

(3) They said hurtful things to one other.

(4) They felt unloved.

(5) They felt taken for granted.

(6) They lacked someone to confide in.

(7) Each spouse felt he or she was giving more than the other.

(8) They rarely complimented each other.

(9) They desired more affection.

(10) They couldn't talk to each other.

Since God performed the first marriage, talking to God about yours would be a good place to start. [66]"

Make a decision that none of the above will be a part of your behaviour and to speak when your interpretation is different from the other: TALK TO EACH OTHER; maybe God as well. It will make a world of difference. For example, your belief about loving the other may not be felt by the other. They may have a different interpretation of the meaning of what you are doing. "Ain't LOVE grand!" Learn to celebrate it and enjoy the frustrations it may bring. Resolving them will lead to an even deeper commitment and joy in your relationship. The decision made in your mind rather than an emotional or physical one is the final and necessary commitment to the other as it is to Christ. It means that all determinate decisions about the relationship will be made in the mind rather than elsewhere. When the head takes over from all other, then the

---

[66] The Word For Today is found at https://vision. org. au/the-word-for-today/

strongest possibilities of a long-term deepening of the relationship are created[67]. (Pity I did not know this years ago!)

It may seem that I have placed too much responsibility on the husband for the success of the relationship. This is not my intention at all. I merely point out ways in which both partners can get more out of the relationship if the man takes a leadership role in honouring, complimenting and affirming his wife. It can be of mutual benefit if the wife assumes a similar role.

And you women! . . . .

Are you one of those who manipulates your husband because you must always get what you want; who uses sex as the means of getting what you want and that you "fake it" so he feels he has done a good job and will therefore be more easily manipulated? You too are missing out. Neither of you are getting anything like what is so readily possible from your relationship. Your best benefit is if you both are open and honest in all aspects of your relationship: that you ask him what he likes you doing; that he asks you what you like and that each of you tell the other when they do something

---

[67] This does not challenge the understandings that the enneagram provides. The way in which one gets to the point of making that intellectual decision will vary from person to person. I suggest that it is the final decision that is in the intellectual domain.

really nice. That way you can both benefit from creative experimentation and learn more and more how you can give pleasure to the one you love and with whom you want to spend the rest of your life.

It might be pertinent here to quote a few of the Proverbs written by the man many consider the wisest who ever lived.

Proverbs 21:9

Better to dwell in a corner of a housetop, than in a house shared with a contentious woman.

Proverbs 11:22

Like a gold ring in a pig's snout is a beautiful woman who shows no discretion.

I realise there are always two points of view to any situation. I include the following as thought provoking for all of us who have made the marriage commitment.

And some really stirring words for men:

Proverbs 5:18-19

18 Let your fountain be blessed,

And rejoice with the wife of your youth.

19 As a loving deer and a graceful doe,

Let her breasts satisfy you at all times;

And always be enraptured with her love.

And a very useful piece of readily accessible advice:

Ephesians 4:27

'Don't let the sun go down while you are still angry, for anger gives a foothold to the devil.' [68]

We need to remember that Paul is writing in the culture of the First Century. That he should suggest that men give honour and respect to their wives was probably quite radical for the time. People will make what they will of what they read and I have no control over what you might think. I will be content if men simply observe Peter's advice in every part:

1 Peter 3:7 NLT

Here's God's plan: '. . . she is your equal partner in God's gift of new life. Treat her as you should, so your prayers will not be hindered.'

Proverbs 31 Also is a description of Solomon's perception of what a woman can be. It begins

"An excellent wife who can find?

She is far more precious than jewels."

No way there is any suggestion a woman is less

---

[68] Some very useful additional references can be found in: 1 Corinthians 13 and Ephesians 5:21-33.

than a man in any way here. Anyone who suggests the Bible is sexist has been misled. What is more, you do not have to be a Christian to read the best source of guidance on how to live your life. So much of what the self-development/personal growth "gurus" purvey has already been written in the Bible, particularly the Gospels. That is a lot cheaper source of guidance for your life!

Unfortunately, my symptoms have progressed and I have had to move into a nursing home. I was offered a place in what might well be the best place in Australia. I chose it immediately. Again, it was unfortunate that my wife was unable to drive there because she had lost the confidence to drive beyond her well-known suburbs and to the other side of the city. The separation seems to be becoming more than due to my ill health since I am unable to do better than use the phone to keep in contact. I suspect that I have also chosen the place because there is an unconscious awareness that I needed to be separate to protect my own health; the relationship had been becoming too stressful for me to manage anymore. (Stress is the cause of worsening symptoms.) So, it would seem that the marriage I had made lasted only six years. Vows were not able to be kept. Another good reason to avoid MS, as if you can. Her desires have been able to be met in ways that might have been thought unimaginable.

Further, the campaign to make men responsible for long past outrageous behaviour seems to be gathering strength with quite a number of high-profile men being brought to account. I recall a conversation I had with a woman whose voice was quite exceptional. (It was before The Bill Cosby and Rolf Harris trials.) She did not pursue a professional career even when it was offered simply because she did not want to play the game of the casting couch to get the roles she deserved or was seeking; sexual immorality was not a part of her acceptable future. I applauded her decision and remarked that I hoped that expectation would soon be removed and merit would be the sole criteria. One might consider that there might be a significant deterrent now, which is added to a more thoughtful and respectful set of values embraced by all genders.

Encounters with God

These encounters occurred along the way as many of the previous *"Musings . . "* were developed. Others might see these experiences in a different light. I am quite convinced that God was acting to influence my thinking or the events themselves.

Several years passed after the Evangelist experience with no significant change. I spoke to God often when I was on my own and listened little; I had no idea of the need to do so. So, life went on, God patiently waiting for me to make the next step or do something different again.

Perhaps the most important, and painful in its retelling, encounter I had with God occurred when I was stopped from committing suicide. I had become very depressed because I was unable to achieve the financial rewards I wanted through the different career I had entered in telecommunications sales. The mortgage repayments were not being made, utilities payments were late, if made at all and I felt it was all my fault and the responsibilities I had taken on, as a husband and father were just not being met. I was an abject failure. My health future was bleak as there was no cure for MS and the symptoms continued to get worse and become more varied.

That does not even begin to capture the way I was feeling at the time. So I don't become repetitive about how absolutely rotten I felt, suffice it to say that it was the darkest period of my life and there was nothing bright in my future that I could see.

My superannuation would clear the debts and provide some funds to allow my wife to make alternative arrangement and I would not be the burden that I saw myself fast becoming as the MS progressed.

I had finished writing the letters to my wife, each of my children, my mother and my siblings on my computer. I saved each of those files and set up a careful means of ensuring the letters would be read by the intended recipient. The means of my demise were very clear and did not include the use of a rope or a cliff. I will not provide those details here. I was ready and quite settled on my abbreviated future as being the best solution for all concerned.

I stood up from my desk and started to move into the last few hours of my life, I thought, pleased I had come to this resolution and with the letters I had written.

Something stopped me: I had more to do. I had no idea what but that was the understanding that hit me as I was about to begin the steps necessary to end all possibility of achieving anything. I can only explain that understanding as coming from God since I was quite settled on my terminal course of action. Now I am grateful beyond any understanding for the life I have now and have had since that time. While my journey to God had not even consciously begun at that time, I look back now and see the experience as being a clear reason to praise and be grateful to Him. An important addition to this story is that, at that realisation of there being more to do, my wife appeared......

A year or so later, my wife and I had reached a point in our relationship which seemed to require my withdrawal for a time. I was supposed to make some realisations about changing my behaviour and becoming a better father/husband or something. I did not understand what really was the problem. It was expected that I would move out over the Easter weekend.

I could not.

I spent the whole weekend vomiting or retching once my stomach was empty. The spasms came every half hour and through the night as well. In those periods when my focus was not consumed with turning myself inside out, I had many thoughts. I came to the conclusions that I had to sing and also go to church.

On the Tuesday after Easter, I rang my friend and asked her where she and her new husband went to church. She responded not only with the name of the church but also with the offer to have her husband collect and take me. This he did and I went to church for a normal service for the first time since I was a teenager. The moment I walked into the foyer I had the feeling that I was HOME.

I also joined the Harmony choir in Adelaide and the first piece I did with them was *The Messiah!*[69]

During the next few months when I felt so totally lost and alone because of my absence from my wife and children, there was huge development in my consciousness and faith. I joined in with a group to complete the Alpha course for people wanting to know more about being a Christian, I was taken on a *Walk To Emmaus*[70] and was lining up to be baptised. My wife stopped that with the communication that if I were to be baptised, I could forget about coming home. I will be forever grateful to the Pastor of the church who wisely

---

[69] The Messiah by G. F. Handel. Considered one of the classic works for choir and soloists. It is performed every year at least once in every capital city in Australia.

[70] Within numerous churches there is a contact who is a member of the group who run a number of different programs for prisoners, teenagers and other audiences. *The Walk to Emmaus* is the primary focus.

suggested that it did not really matter since I had been baptised in the spirit anyway and the sacrament could wait until a better time.

During this period of estrangement, my mother became sicker and sicker with cancer and I spent a week with her at the family home overlooking the Torrens Valley. During that week the famous fogs were as beautiful as they have ever been, filling the whole valley with the sun streaming down onto it from a cloudless sky. One of the best things from her point of view was that I was able to pray with her for Jesus to come and take her home to be with Him. I felt quite distressed at her imminent death and derived considerable comfort from her faith and mine.

Naturally, after Mum's death, my wife and children came to the funeral and I spent the evening with them. I was staying with one of my brothers at the time and made the lengthy drive from one side of Adelaide to the other, probably inadvisably as I was stopped by a policeman who gave me a breath test. When that was quite clear, his comment was that he had never seen anybody drive so haphazardly without them being drunk: I was really struggling to stay awake. The remainder of my journey was made with the window down and the radio blaring to keep me awake. I made it safely. Thank God.

* * *

In retrospect, this was one of many occasions where God has been my protector in circumstances where I have not been on top of what I have been doing and events transpired which were of extreme danger. I escaped without a scratch from all of them.

I outline a number of other experiences, mainly in the order in which they occurred but there is not any other apparent connection between them.

* * *

I had moved to Cairns with the expectation that I would be entering a long-term relationship only to discover that my expectations were totally misplaced. I had really made a mess of what might have been a wonderful extension of our experiences together as a result. Nonetheless, I had moved to Cairns and chose to explore what it might show me about life. One of the suggestions that were made is that I see a healer on the Atherton Tablelands who had been responsible for a woman losing her symptoms of MS after a lengthy period of treatment. I sought to follow that path and began travelling up the Gillies Highway every fortnight for treatment.

Wikipedia describes the Gillies Highway thus: "Famous for its 263 corners, and 800 m elevation change in only 19 km of road". This was no road to be treated lightly with an almost sheer drop on one side to the bottom of the range and a cliff that had been cut into the steep slope on the other.

One day it was very wet and I was travelling too fast. I avoided the cliff . . . and went over the edge.

Given my lack of stamina for any physical activity, I did well to get to within a few metres of the top. It took about two hours to attract the attention of a passing motorist because I was over the side and out of view. My shouts finally penetrated an open window of a passing vehicle and I was rescued as a result.

My manual car was a write-off and the insurance pay-out enabled me to buy another car with some assistance. A couple that I had met at the church later looked at the spot where I had gone over and were amazed I had survived. The car had careered down the slope, knocking over a small pine tree and passing between two very large rocky outcrops, each of which was larger than the car. It had come to rest against a large gum tree, having destroyed a lot of vegetation on the way down, thereby reducing the final impact. I was later to interpret the event as a wake up from God and a reminder that God had things for me to do.

It was also the case that it was becoming necessary to drive an automatic car so that my left leg was not required to operate the clutch.

*   *   *

I had entered into a new relationship and we were sharing rental accommodation. The intimate relationship ended although the friendship did not. My friend made a trip to Western Australia and returned with her adult son. The unit we shared was not big enough for three of us even though we persevered. Living conditions were not really acceptable as my friend slept in the living room on the large settee. It was becoming more and more difficult in those circumstances. I had made application to Queensland Housing and then was offered a **brand-new unit** in a block that had been **built for disabled** people particularly. I accepted and moved in immediately it could be arranged. Everything I needed appeared just as I became aware of its necessity. My brand-new unit was set up very well and I could buy from the Op Shop those few necessary items that had not been provided as gifts by others. I had several years there until I returned to Adelaide to marry my new wife, as described a little later in this chapter. It was a very happy period of my time in Cairns and I thank God for the circumstances in which I was offered it. I know that Queensland Housing is in the business of providing housing for people who are in difficult circumstances. Nonetheless, I am grateful for all that was provided.

It was there that I spent the night when cyclone Yasi was expected to cross the coast right at Cairns. Fortunately for all the tens of thousands of people who lived there, it made a left turn some 50 kms off the coast and wrecked the smaller communities further south. I hope I never have to experience another cyclone, although I know I will be safe, regardless. It was a most exciting night with little sleep as the wind and rain battered us, even 50 kms from its centre. The huge damage to the communities further south and to the vegetation in the Cairns area was monstrous.

*   *   *

At one stage I was being challenged by a dull ache in my left ankle that was keeping me awake at night. The doctor described it as neuropathic pain. This is not uncommon in people with MS and I had been very fortunate until then with none of that as a symptom. As a result of reduced sleep, I was developing worse symptoms of poorer mobility and balance and greater fatigue. I was becoming pretty cross about the situation. One night I had gone to sleep and then been woken by the need to go to the toilet (very common symptom). When I went back to bed, I was unable to sleep or get comfortable. I sat on the edge of my bed and had a few very strong words to say. I was angry and vented that anger towards God in very strong language, saying that God could do something about it if God wanted to and God knew my predicament of needing sleep. I heard a voice say quite clearly, "Don't worry! Go back to bed. Everything is alright." I grumbled back under the sheet and the next thing I knew it was morning; six hours later.

Getting to sleep has seldom been a problem since.

*   *   *

I had struggled with money all my life, never having quite enough even when I was earning very well as a Senior Teacher and then as Acting Deputy Principal. It was even harder when my sole income became the Disability Support Pension. I had read and been told about tithing and felt that I could not possibly afford to give away ten per cent of my income. In the Bible there are a number of discussions about tithing. One of them says, "Test me in this"[71]. I decided to do so and over the next 12 months at least and thereafter I have had no shortage of funds to do any of the things I needed to do or perhaps God had in mind that I should. At least the following expenses were met on my behalf during the ensuing twelve months.

I flew from Cairns to the Gold Coast and back so I could spend some time with a new friend.

I bought a new electric scooter, at a heavily discounted price.

I flew to Adelaide and back for family reasons.

All bills were paid on receipt of the account or soon after.

And there was more that I cannot recall as I am

---

[71] Malachi 3:10 (NIV)

writing this. My gratitude is extreme in my expression for all that God has done for me in all aspects of my life, even to the diagnosis of MS since I have learned so much from having it that I would not have done had I not been diagnosed.

Thank you, God for everything.

*   *   *

One instance of provision is noteworthy as it was so unexpected. Early in the period after my decision to tithe, I was still dubious that it really worked until the following events occurred.

I had spent all of my available funds and had miscalculated what I thought I needed to get me through to the next payday. I came to accept that there would be one meal short if I made my usual donation to the church. I knew that $10 was the amount I really needed to get me through.

I had been trying to increase my income with a multi-level marketing opportunity that involved selling a product that was demonstrably of benefit to at least some people. I had virtually given up, as it required the expenditure of energy that I did not have. Out of the blue, a potential customer, long forgotten as being a possibility, rang me and ordered $10 worth of the product. I would eat all of the scheduled meals until payday after all. Thanks God.

*　　　*　　　*

One morning I woke and washed my face and went in to read the "Word for Today"[72]. I found that the words I was looking at became invisible and the only way I could read was to look in the near vicinity of the words I was reading. This was not a new experience since each of my eyes have been totally blind at one stage and have recovered. I went and washed my face again, thinking that it might be some stray "sleep" residue causing the problem.

No change.

I prayed, "Lord, I cannot read your Word unless I can see."

Within seconds my vision was clear and I went on to read the whole of the readings for the day, praising God as I did so.

I am so joyful to be a child of God and know

---

[72] Bob and Debbie Gass wrote "The Word For Today" with a selection of texts from the Bible. The effect is to read the whole Bible in a year. I use the on-line facility they provide.

God's love. I repeat the prayer whenever the problem with my sight returns. That has been quite seldom.

*   *   *

Simple solutions are always the best. They need to be looked for first before engaging the "professionals" and paying them lots of money to find a complex and time-wasting solution. Its a bit like life; seeing the counsellor, psychologist and even psychiatrist when the simple solution is to pray, fervently and in the belief that an answer will be provided. Whenever I feel a bit down, I simply pray and ask God to show me what I need to do if anything. The answer always comes, most often in the form of a visit to the rainforest to be reminded of what beauty God has given me to enjoy and then I am reminded of the glorious life which awaits when this one is finished and I have done all that God wanted me to do.

The simple solution is Faith that Grace is poured out for us all. We just need to accept it; gleefully, knowing that God is our friend, protector, saviour and provider of all we need.

That came on me as I was sitting here. Tell me that God is not part of my life and I will laugh. There is so much joy available for us all. Praising God provides us with huge benefits.

This is amazing. I am not even thinking: just writing. Joy and love for God is bubbling out of me as I sit here. I read the beginning of Acts this morning as part of *The Word For Today*. Maybe that is the instigator. I really don't care. Either way, God has a hand in my joy at this moment when I had been feeling a bit off about my future. Who cares when I have God with me to comfort me and hold my hand?

*   *   *

Sometimes it only needs some common sense to get things going...

You don't have to be an engineer to appreciate this story. I only include it because it shows that there are simple solutions when we ask God and look for them rather than to make things complicated.

A toothpaste factory had a problem. They sometimes shipped empty boxes without the tube inside. This challenged their perceived quality with the buyers and distributors. Understanding how important the relationship with them was, the CEO of the company assembled his top people.

They decided to hire an external engineering company to solve their empty boxes problem. The project followed the usual process: budget and project sponsor allocated, RFP, and third parties selected. Six months (and $8 million) later they had a fantastic solution - on time, on budget, and high quality. Everyone in the project was pleased.

They solved the problem by using a high-tech precision scale that would sound a bell and flash lights whenever a toothpaste box weighed less than it should. The line would stop; someone would walk over, remove the defective box and then press another button to re-start the line. As a result of the new package monitoring process, no empty boxes were being shipped out of the factory.

With no more customer complaints, the CEO felt the $8 million was well spent. He then reviewed the line statistics report and discovered the number of empty boxes picked up by the scale in the first week was consistent with projections. However, the next three weeks were zero! The estimated rate should have been at least a dozen boxes a day. The CEO had the engineers check the equipment; they verified the report as accurate.

Puzzled, the CEO went down to the factory, viewed the part of the line where the precision scale was installed and observed just ahead of the new $8 million dollar solution sat a $20 desk fan blowing the empty boxes off the belt and into a bin. He asked the line supervisor what that was about.

"Oh, that," the supervisor replied, "Bert, the kid from maintenance, put it there because he was tired of walking over, removing the box and re-starting the line every-time the bell rang."

A similar story relates to the development of a ballpoint pen that would work in the weightless environment of space. The USA spent many dollars and much time while the Russians used a pencil!

*   *   *

I had spent some months writing some of the contents of this book when I was approached by an acquaintance from about ten years before who asked me to assist him "knock into shape what he had already written as an account of his being defrauded and impoverished". He estimated the time would be no more than two or three months. I spent some time in prayer asking for guidance as to whether I should be involved and received the response that I should. We finished a satisfactory, published book three and a half years later, after many additions to the text and subjects discussed!

At every point, we felt that there was a presence making things happen the way they did. It always turned out that there was a significant improvement to the overall content as a result. One of the most amazing events was my co-author coming across a laser printer on the footpath, just left there. It has meant that we have been able to look at the layout of the text so it can be set up for best effect when preparing for the printer. It also means we can print copies of the book and, with the dexterous use of a glue gun, bind it as well. It is not an ordinary laser printer and provides for very rapid printing of large volumes of copies.

That time extended when we decided that a cheaper format and serious edit would be of benefit in making the book and therefore its contents more accessible. It stretched to more than four years and other issues arose that delayed the publication of the finished product. We remain confident that the product we eventually make available will be excellent and well received.[73]

*   *   *

---

[73] The books referred to are *Phoenix Activity Report* and *Corruption Crisis*".

The last story is about a new relationship, leading to marriage, which developed over the Internet. I decided it would be good to enter a new marital relationship with a person who shared my faith. I enrolled on a dating site since the women that I had met in Cairns did not spark the interest needed for such a relationship. There was a woman in Adelaide who was of a similar mind who also had been enrolled on that dating site by a friend, determined to assist her in her goal. Her search parameters were set to within fifty kilometres of Adelaide.

I showed up! In Cairns! About 3000 kms away!

We made contact and our first conversation on Skype lasted for six and a half hours. At 3.30 am I suggested that it was time we went to bed. Then I thought about what I had said and laughed. Not much chance of going to bed together when she was in Adelaide and I was in Cairns. Nonetheless, we shared many meals and hours on Skype together and exchanged visits. All of that led to our marriage in Adelaide some five and a half months later. Both of us were looking for a Christian partner and we found each other, as some might say by chance. I prefer to say that God had something to do with that change to her search parameters. I am originally from Adelaide and had left it after I left my marriage. I came back to marry my lovely wife and to be near my two adult children and most of my siblings. The way it all worked out was wonderful. Life goes on together, with the bumps in the road that happen. They become manageable with God.

It was also the case that I paid for two return flights and a one-way flight from Cairns to Adelaide and then both of us returned to Cairns for a month the next year, all from resources that appeared just at the right time. Thanks God! (I live with only the Disability Support Pension as my income. I rely on God for the rest. It seems to appear as needed.)

My daily routine includes some time reading extracts from the Bible as part of a prayer routine. I have found it of real benefit as I am reminded of my gratitude for all that God has provided; the Bible gives me much joy as I read it every day, nearly.

My encounters with God and God's Son Jesus are wonderful. I can only continue in praise and thanksgiving. There is so much Joy as a result of God's Grace and Love. I continue to grow with Jesus in every step of my way.

Perhaps the most important revelation for me concerns "salvation". It is the salvation which is available HERE and NOW, not so much after death, that is most important to me and maybe

you. Death and what comes after is something which, like tomorrow, has enough concerns for itself. I can do little about that now. What is important is that we can be forgiven and saved from further punishment in our own minds that really counts in this life we are living. That provides so much freedom; knowing we are saved from our own mistakes and misdeeds. Just like that miscreant, king David, who wrote so many of the psalms. It is enough for me to live in the knowledge that Jesus and God have the future well in hand. Praise the Lord!

How wonderful is that?

Epilogue

That blinding flash of the prologue was one of **mis-**understanding, not understanding.

Strange how God gets God's way, in spite of us. Best we get in step with what God has in mind so it happens without the struggles of conflict.

What have I learned?

1. We don't really have much say in life. I have mucked up one of the most important parts of my life through not following the best advice around.
2. I accept that I have to take responsibility for all that I have done and do, always. Better get God involved a lot more so stupid decisions are not made.
3. If I want more I best give more; in every part of my life. That certainly applies to relationships as well as to the financial rewards to be had at least.
4. Find something which really "rocks your boat", "turns you on', "gives you a buzz", that you are really good at and then devote your life to it, wholeheartedly. All that you need will come when it is needed; sometimes only just in time. Be patient, yet make sure you really love it; or the other person.
5. How to make a bed and some other things 'right the first time'.
6. The Bible has so much information for living and it is very easily found with the help of the search engine technology we have now.

Having God as a big part of your life will make it so much easier and better.

Poems

My Loving Prayer

Vernon Lewis

I am so grace-filled and grateful
For the love in my life.
That you should show me what two people can share
And drown in the joyful love they create,
When all of the soul is laid bare
It's all of the person that is stripped to become raw
And tender together with care.
The deep-seated joy felt by both of us
Is shocking and shattering;
Give me more.
And more of the same or better
Is the only way forward from here.
That you should show me what two people can share.
I am so grace-filled and grateful
For the love in my life.
Only grace knows what is to come.
Grace knows it is for our best.

2007

Headlights in the Sky
Vernon Lewis

Intended as a performance piece, the different fonts in the second part being different characters

Headlights in the sky
What anxieties are **here**?
What is this apparition
Sneaking in the clouds
and darkening sky?
What could it be?
We're sipping our wine and eating our fish
Al fresco in the evening
On the deck over lapping water
No aberrations please!
What on Earth (or off it) can it be?
The headlights, coming nearer
Flanked by other lights, well spread
And under another, flashing

It's a plane!

Headlights in the sky. What anxieties are **there?**
As the seatbelt sign says "fasten"
And the crew are sitting, strapped ready for landing

I'm not scared. No-one will see me in fear
The pilots know their stuff.
They wouldn't ever dare with me on board, to stuff up a simple landing
In weather fine and fair

Dear God, Guide the hands of the pilots
As they carry out this highly responsible task.
Bring us all safe to Earth to the homes of our loved ones
Who are safe on the ground. Amen

If my number is up, Its up
I'll just sit here and read my book until its time to leave
Unbuckle my belt and
Clear the overhead locker before the crowd
So I get off the quickest and am gone. No waiting for me:
I'm special

Headlights on the ground
The plane lands safely
Like every other time, ...
So far

2007

You and Me
Vernon Lewis

Whence comes this feeling of boundless love
Of joyful acceptance of whatever is
When doubts arise, all is washed clear
And all is joyfully loving still
The passion is just a small part of this love
Which brings to life feelings of genuine warmth
Of traditional roles of men being strong
Protectors, providers and tender, considerate leaders
The heart is so full of joyful abandon
Both give each other the tribute of surrender
Words cannot make sufficient expression
To the feelings bursting from the heart
I Love You

2008

I can stay here no longer

Vernon Lewis

I can stay here no longer; I've done all I can
To love as you want, to be what you want
To live like you need, to change who I am
To be loved as I want, to feel I'm OK
There's got to be a way of being with someone
Where we say what we mean and are understood
Understood what is said, understood what is done
Understand what is said and done and not judged
No longer can I continue the lie of fidelity
In the face of prejudgement, rejection
And a decision already made.
So, I'll leave with a heart filled with sadness
The efforts have been made; the tears have been shed
The lingering pain recurs again and again
With a new understanding and faith
To be open and honest and free
I go into the world and the pain disappears
Joy re-appears and a deeper love arises
There is Joy in the sharing of the ways of Grace
With gratefulness. I am so happy to be free (and in love)

2008

Walls

Vernon Lewis

I grieve to see your struggle, your fear
Your splashing in the water
That drives the lifebuoy clear
Where came these walls?
Where once was ease and light
Where all just turned out right.
Now nothing is easy, nothing right.
Where we rejoiced in each other
It's now just so much bother
If we cannot share, rejoice in each other
At least you need not have this care
That drowns you, all a smother
Constant struggle sees you always tired
Incapable of seeing where to go,
What to do
But it's really all too much
Love yourself and live your life
Don't know what that is?
Trust the opportunities will come
Thank you for being the wonderful person you really are
The joy we shared was its own reward, Thank you.
If walls it is then at least be free of all this "efforting".

2008

Road to Copperlode Dam

Vernon Lewis

Canopy over all shuts out the sky but not the afternoon light.
Vine-bearded trees filter sunbeams
Shedding everywhere a golden glow
In ravines shaping the road.
Occasional birdcalls break the silence...
Unwelcome views between the trees of the nearby city
Remind how close this glory is to those who stop to stare
At the view of man-made buildings when
Nature is the opposite direction and
Waiting, lover-like to be appreciated for what she offers.
Lake Morris glistens man-made in the
Rainforest covered surrounds and islands.
Proximity is wasted on those who see the beauty as mundane
Perhaps it takes a visitor to see
Reality of what is freely here
And in need of care and nurturing, not progress raping
How can this glorious nature live on beyond our lives?
Grow stronger and more beauteous with the passing years
Not less and smaller as more is removed

CAN WE STOP DESTRUCTION OF SUCH BEAUTY?

I can only write telling others and hope they do not come
To build new houses where there is no room
On the rainforest stabilised skittering scree
Straining further this fragile, caressing landscape

2008

Gillies Highway

Vernon Lewis

I had gone over the edge the year before, . . . not carefully

Cloud shadowed Piebald Green-blue rainforest
Carpets a huge amphitheatre of view below and before
Mist on the mountains behind
The road a treacherous and bewitching journey
Of views and seventeen kilometres of S-bends
No safety rail, huge drops all along the left
Danger at every turn, glorious views distract
And slippery when wet.
A journey well worth making . . . carefully

2009

Lines at sundown looking over Atherton

Vernon Lewis

Clouds sit on the mountains as Sun sets behind.
Vapour filtered rays bathe the rainforest slopes
In a golden glow.
Warmth turns to refreshing chill
And a warmer top than a T-shirt.
There is promise of morning as Sun sets
At the upper wisps of clouds
Then relaxes to the inevitable.
Dusk turns swiftly to dark
As the town lights come alive.

2009

In Church, 25/01/09

Vernon Lewis

Life is an emptiness
A space not filled with sense.
(Long is it since I sought for sense)
Some days are just too long
And NEVER get to bedtime.
And yet there is a goal,
It seems just out of reach.
Is that the goal worth striving for
Or is it misled belief?
So just surrender to the Love
That's free to all who seek it.
I have less of my life left
Than has already passed.
My faith feels strong
But somehow empty.

I am in need of reconnecting
To joy and freedom
Clarity and confidence . . . .

GOD . . . . . .

LOVE . . . .

"All we need is Love"
Is the anthem sung in a different space
But true for all no less.
Surrender to God offered Love
Let Him create your life
And live in God's freedom.

Be prepared to hang on tight.

                        2009

Ode to the sheet

Vernon Lewis

I really needed to buy a new sheet . . .

Such a simple thing,
An old sheet torn needing a new
Purchase made at bargain price
Value three times that paid.

Yet not replaced for three days
Am I not worthy of the new?
The crisp new cloth, smooth on mattress
Vastly better than split and frayed
Thin to just cover the mattress, nearly

This is metaphor for the way I lived
Procrastinating, delaying most important change
For a better life in all respects
Shabby self concept like the sheet

I choose a bed, smooth and clean
The wrinkles signs of familiar comfort

From pleasant sleeping occupation
And fruitful dreaming of masterful change

I take control of my life in all respects
To accept responsibility for all

Whatever it is and was
There is no need to wait
It is already whole
In all respects, love, wealth and health
And nature of accommodation

The past is gone,
Cannot be undone.
The present is all that is
The power is now, the future will be what will is when it comes
Be what it is that I am

Let this sheet be an ongoing lesson
Of esteem that will not lessen
For me as I make the life
I decide is that which is right for me
I love me enough to choose my life
The way I want it to be
And live it as of now

Hallelujah, for the sheet

2009

Metaphor

Vernon Lewis

To accompany a photo of my son and grandson walking into the sun on a beach

Footprints up and back
Is so much more than that.
A father and his son!
Much love and joy in fact.

The nature of that love
Changes as they grow
The son learns to return
The love his father showed.

The love becomes much more
Than just between the two.
It spreads beyond the door
As the son begins to grow.

And Grandpa is so touched,
To see it all pass on.
The beach walk is redone
And love is passed along

2017

www.ingramcontent.com/pod-product-compliance
Lightning Source LLC
Chambersburg PA
CBHW030038100526
44590CB00011B/253